ADVANCE PRAISE FOR

Standstill

"A charming and wise book, a book of humble thought and good talk. These meditations blend points of view and moments of awareness with ease across time, cultures, and species. The resulting wholeness, formed out of awkward human life, is graceful and extraordinary."

—HAROLD RHENISCH, author of *Salmon Shanties* and *The Art of Haying: A Journey to Iceland*

"I've long admired the breadth of Bruce Rice's sophisticated poetry, and now, with *Standstill,* I can attest that his creative nonfiction is equally diverse—and even more satisfying. This is Rice on pilgrimage: the precise observations of and gentle engagement with birds and 'maples illuminated in their autumn haloes'; the intimate confessions and surprising ironies; the tenderness of a brother signing 'slow' on his deaf sister's wrist as she struggles in hospital to breathe. *Standstill* is a collection one experiences and this exemplary writer's finest book to date."

—SHELLEY A. LEEDAHL, author of *Go, I Wasn't Always Like This,* and *Listen, Honey*

"Bruce Rice's carefully crafted essays take us deeper into what it is to be a brother, a friend, an artist in a fragmented world."

—TREVOR HERRIOT, author of *The Economy of Sparrows* and *Towards a Prairie Atonement*

Standstill

A Hopewell Earthworks Daybook and Other Essays

Bruce Rice

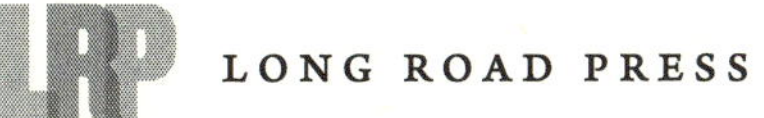
LONG ROAD PRESS

Printed and bound in Canada. The text of this book is printed on 100% post-consumer recycled paper with earth-friendly vegetable-based inks.

COVER PHOTO NAND SECTION PHOTOS: "Standing on a Hill, 1999."
Photo by Barbara Bosworth. Reproduced with permission.
COVER AND TEXT DESIGN: Duncan Noel Campbell
COPY EDITOR / PROOFREADER: Kelly Laycock
EDITOR: Brian Bartlett

Library and Archives Canada Cataloguing in Publication

TITLE: Standstill : a Hopewell Earthworks daybook and other essays / Bruce Rice.

NAMES: Rice, Bruce, author

DESCRIPTION: Includes bibliographical references.

IDENTIFIERS: Canadiana (print) 20240476174 | Canadiana (ebook) 20240476212 | ISBN 9781068949708 (softcover) | ISBN 9781068949715 (EPUB)

SUBJECTS: Rice, Bruce—Travel—Ohio River—Diaries. | LCSH: Hopewell culture—Ohio. | LCSH: Earthworks (Archaeology)—Ohio. | LCSH: Art and society. | LCSH: Disabilities. | LCSH: Ohio River—Description and travel. | LCGFT: Diaries. | LCGFT: Essays.

CLASSIFICATION: LCC PS8585.I128 Z46 S2024 | DDC C811/.54—dc23

10 9 8 7 6 5 4 3 2 1

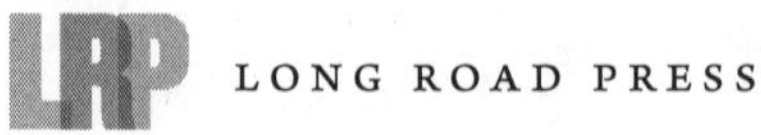

The author gratefully acknowledges Access Copyright Foundation and SK Arts for support for travel to the Hopewell Earthworks in 2017 and 2019.

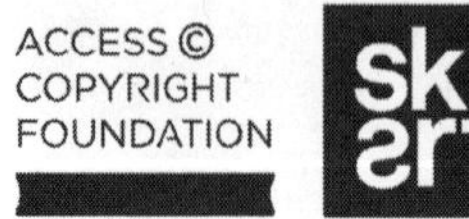

In memory of my parents, Greg Rice, whose books
I grew up with, and my mother, Pearl,
an every-night, all-night reader.

And to absent friends, Barbara Bauche and Byrna Barclay.

Contents

Foreword

I call myself a poet. Mostly. So, it feels right that this collection begins with a memoir inspired by the Japanese form known as *utanikki,* the thousand-year-old tradition of the poetic travel journal.[1] The "Hopewell Earthworks Daybook" in Part 1 is a daily journal of my travels among the two-thousand-year-old Native American earthworks built along tributaries of the Ohio River. I'll leave the improbable story of how I got there to the journal itself. I needed to ask how a person like me, who isn't Indigenous, can respond authentically to these works and what they transmit—the imagination, the science, and the ways of being behind them. The Ohio journey also made me ask how much I know of the land just outside my door—these Northern Great Plains, which are old and the colour of tallow for much of the year. Then they renew. The deep past when we were less apart seems like a good place to begin.

"Little Voices" in Part 2 is a reflection on the many people I have known who have challenges with speech or who have lost the power of speech entirely. It starts with my sister Anne, who is deaf and had to learn to speak all over again; others spent part or all of their lives in institutions. I've known people like this since I was a child. And one was a poet. They were fighters because they had to be. Their stories recounted here are also about identity—mine as much as theirs. They are personal to me, but they are also part of a social history that is still largely invisible.

How many times has some Google-prone scribbler glibly quoted that famous W.H. Auden line, "poetry makes nothing happen"? Perhaps I should say *misquote,* because one wonders if they read the whole poem. "Song of the Lark" in Part 3 is inspired by art that has literally saved lives. Individual lives, and sometimes hundreds of lives. Works like these are their own proof of the force of art—in our hearts and in our actions. As for the adventures of Buzzy the Kamikaze Rabbit (Part 4), I can only say that the operative part of the phrase "creative nonfiction" is the word *nonfiction*. As the saying goes, you can't make this stuff up.

"Silence, A Brother's Journal" at the end of the book was written at my sister Anne's bedside in the intensive care unit of a Dartmouth, Nova Scotia hospital. It was a battle with pneumonia that the doctors didn't expect her to win. Much of her life is still missing from me. From the age of five, she spent years away in schools for the deaf in other cities. Then came university and how families drift away from each other through distance and who we are. I started the journal so that, whether she survived or not, at least that experience wouldn't be taken away as well. Those sixteen days changed both our lives, making a space for ordinary things put off for so long.

Writing about Anne taught me about something I thought was lost. It still surprises me. In "Little Voices" and "Song of the Lark," art and writing and music cut through the noise—affirming the best part of ourselves, the inspiring part, and the unspoken courage that's more common than we think. As for what the Hopewell people built, Greg Johnson an advocate for sacred land struggles, says that these kinds of sites can be "owned" and cared for through story—by which he means the kinds of stories that move and grow communities through their telling.[2] The daybook and essays that follow are offered in this spirit—and as a reflection on the sum of the human spaces we share.

This project would not have been possible without the help, advice, and generosity of many individuals and organizations in Canada and the United States. They are noted with gratitude in the Acknowledgements section. I have tried to work in a way that respects the traditions and life experience of the people(s) in the pages that follow. Any fault is purely my own. Some names have been changed for reasons of privacy.

Bruce Rice, Regina, Saskatchewan
Treaty 4 Territory and homeland of the Métis Nation

PART 1

Hopewell Earthworks Daybook

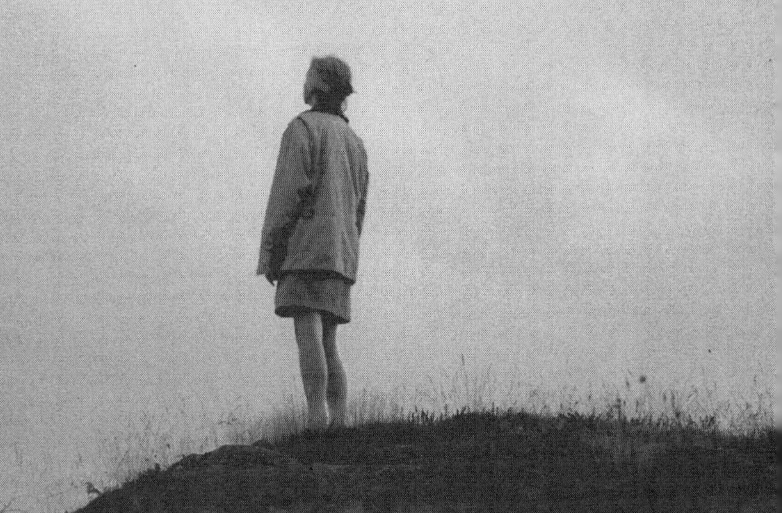

THE MAJOR LUNAR STANDSTILL

The moon completes a remarkable cycle every 18.6 years. Over this time, the moon in its travels will reach its most northerly point in the night sky at about 28° above the equator. This is due to the gradual northward shift in the angle of its orbit around the Earth. What ancient peoples observed from hilltops, we call the major lunar standstill because it is the "pause" in the moon's northward movement before heading south again.

The Standing Stones of Callanish on the Isle of Lewis, the Stones of Stenness in Orkney, and perhaps other Neolithic sites, are aligned with the major standstill. There are three known Native American standstill sites. The two in the west include Chimney Rock in Colorado's Chaco Canyon and the Sun Dagger 140 miles farther south at Fajada Butte, New Mexico. The third Native American standstill site is the Octagon and Observatory Circle in Newark, Ohio. In January 2025, the standstill cycle will peak as the moon rises once more from the "gate" in the Octagon, 38 degrees north of east, as it has for two thousand years.

ISLE OF LEWIS, OUTER HEBRIDES, SCOTLAND
July 2012

The prairie creature in me is drawn to the farthest edges of a place. I arrived on Isle of Lewis two days ago. I am three hours by ferry and bus from Uig on the tip of Skye, and another hour from Stornoway. North Atlantic wind comes in from the sea loch; the heather holds back its bloom. I walk the worn footpath that passes between the Standing Stones of Callanish. The land is rough like the Canadian Arctic in summer, a mottled skin of soil, terra cotta–coloured lichens, and tough grass that grips the rock where it can. The jet stream has stalled, causing heavy rain and flooding in Scotland and England. This is June, but there are so few people it feels like the end of the season. A low white fence separates the last houses of Callanish village on one side from the annoyance of tourists on the other. I walk the avenue of gneiss-grey stones set in the earth like pieces of fallen sky. They become taller than me on their way up the crest of the hill crowned by a circle of glyphs. The main stone is 4.8 metres high and weighs seven tonnes. I'm not sure I should touch it but finally raise my palm to a slight, rounded protrusion, only to find that it's warm like flesh, not the indifferent cold I was expecting.

> the shoulder
> the weight   the crossing
>
> Little Minch   where Blue Men
> sleep and rumble in undersea caves
> North Minch   the strait

Cliff or hillock or cove, stories grow into their places. Their names become bone names with a resonance even a stranger can feel: a headland; Loch Seaforth, also called *Aird Lamishader* in Gaelic; Callanish becomes *Calanais* or *Gaidhlig*; Isle of Lewis, *Eilean an Fhraoich,* isle of flowers.

> a pull like the Moon
> which is only
> moon in one language
> a not very old one at that

Prairie eyes like sea eyes are made for distances, scanning the horizon for small interruptions. Even in this light, the hills to the south form the silhouette of a woman sleeping. She is pregnant. If I stayed long enough, I would see what has been going on for four thousand years. Every 18.6 years the moon's orbit reaches the farthest point in its slow journey north before reversing its path, travelling south for 9.3 years until the cycle begins again. This "pause" before its journey south is called the major lunar standstill.

When the standstill comes, Luna's arc through the Northern Sky is the widest it will ever be. Her path at Callanish stays so close to the Earth that it barely skims the horizon. It traces the tops of the stones, which in turn align with the form of the sleeping mother and the child inside her. What was built here has to do with harvest or some essential communion: the mystic equilibrium between sun and moon, or the continuance of life itself. Only some great urgency of belief can explain it. In the only place where it could happen, all we have is that word *belief*.

and a name   Calanais
stone but not stone   tonnes of it
a message to the future

ARRIVAL, COLUMBUS, OH

June 2017, first day

I am finally here. If not for the stones on Lewis, I would never have thought to search out one of the three Native American standstill sites a few hours' flight from my home. The Octagon and Observatory Circle an hour from Columbus are part of a series of massive geometric sites built by people of the Hopewell culture two thousand years ago. Unlike the stone monuments of Scotland, or Colorado's Chimney Rock and the Sun Dagger at Fajada Butte, the medium used here was earth. The Hopewell levelled hilltops and built up the walls of their great circles and burial mounds in carefully engineered layers.

The classicist Guy Davenport speculates about the geography of the imagination, the way images like the ones here imprint themselves in memory in indelible forms that follow the human diaspora across the world to be reborn in art and even the shapes of our tools. And yet, the stone circles of Callanish and Stenness in Orkney are separated from what early Native Americans built along tributaries of the Ohio River by twenty centuries and an ocean. There was no contact. I know there are other explanations, but it seems only natural to ask: what if Davenport was only half right? Our imagination travels with us. But what if it travels without us—sailing the Earth on its own wind? This kind of notion goes against everything my social science brain will allow. Call it a conceit and I won't blame you. I expect all this to end in failure anyway. But something in me refuses to abandon such a beautiful question.

> circle or henge, what's the difference   diameter
> two thousand years   or four
> the seeing
>
> somehow it got here or maybe
> here's where it started

The Hopewell people were here between 100 BCE and 500 CE. Many of the earthworks they left us are so monumental in size they can't be seen from a single viewpoint. Even the Native Americans here at first contact didn't know what the builders called themselves. The three-and-a-half-mile hilltop wall at Fort Ancient, the surviving circles 1,100 feet across, and the four-square-mile complex known as the Newark Earthworks show a knowledge of cosmology and the application of geometry over great distances that rivals any in the ancient world.

> Hold on to a peg on a relatively flat field. A friend
> walks around you with a long piece of rope, marking
> the arc, the diameter of circles, right-
> angle intersections. Squares and octagons.
>
> But try to stand on a hill, take a bearing.
> Transpose that bearing to the mark you must now
> make on the valley floor miles below. That's
> something else. Entirely.[1]

I've walked prairie fields looking for arrowheads since I was a kid. Three hours from my home, the St. Victor petroglyphs look north from a high sandstone outcrop that overlooks miles of rolling pasture and cropland. I know a place where you can stand in the worn track next to a rubbing stone smoothed by generations of bison—shaggy, truculent beasts. These marks in the land are a language. I know it only slightly, but I'm not ignorant of it either. One of the most important Hopewell sites allows visitors only four days a year. I've come to see their ceremonial sites and burial mounds and to walk through their gates. I admit to feeling a bit like the seventeenth-century Japanese poet Matsuo Bashō, who wrote in his famous work *The Narrow Road to the Deep North*:

> So that year—the second year of Genroku [1689]—I had suddenly taken it into my head to make the long journey into the deep north, to see with my own eyes places that I had only heard about, despite hardships enough to turn my hair white. I should be lucky to come back alive, but I staked my fortune on that uncertain hope.[2]

Unlike Bashō, I have come south. I didn't sell my possessions. There are no bandits to worry about, just a country I know from TV, airport stopovers, and a few excursions across the border. I don't expect a kind farmer to lend me his horse and send his children along to retrieve it. I rented a car. I chose extra-light footwear—blue runners with soles that roll easily for walking long distances. The style is undistinguished except for the small, fluorescent green flashes on the sides. It's the most I have ever paid for such a thing. Bashō, who appreciated cultivated taste, wrote:

> I will bind iris
> blossoms round my feet—
> straps for my sandals

What I write now comes from the desk of my B&B in Columbus, from an art museum garden, a Carnegie library, and from hilltops and restaurant tables. There's a border town called Peebles with its overheard Ohio and Kentucky accents, and a fifty-dollar motel room in a town called Lebanon. It's an easier journey than Bashō's. No iris sandals, but a pilgrimage all the same. And as I said, it didn't start here.

SCULPTURE GARDEN, COLUMBUS MUSEUM OF ART
morning, second day

It's an easy five-minute drive from my B&B to the Columbus Museum of Art. I came here to think. All I have is the map I printed off at home. I've circled the places I think I should go with a yellow marker, but the map says nothing back and the US highway numbering system means nothing to me. This whole trip could be a disaster. I want to trust the books and the subtle, grass-covered forms laid out on a scale that YouTube videos can't capture. The distances are too great. I'm not sure how to be in a country where everything sees me. I get the seniors rate at the desk. Instead of going upstairs to the exhibits, I head outside to the courtyard I passed on my way in from the parking lot. It's a newly finished sculpture garden screened on three sides by white panel walls. The black reflecting pool has been taken over by grackles that flutter and squawk as they battle for bathing spots. The birds are at ease with Aristide Maillol's partially reclining nude they share the pool with.

I like the light in places like this, what it chooses to valorize and its solitudes. I choose a bench tucked in a pocket of newly inserted trees. A sensor triggers *Study for Strings,* a sound sculpture by Susan Philipsz. It's a reconstruction of the viola and cello parts from a 1943 orchestral work by Pavel Haas. Haas was forced to create the piece for *Theresiendstadt,* the 1944 Nazi propaganda film about the SS concentration camp an hour from Prague. As the film rolls, rows of muscular young men exercise ballet-like in a pan shot of a "model Jewish settlement." Haas and many of the musicians were killed shortly afterward. The silence between the notes recalls the missing in spaces left for something to fall through. I never expected this, I only wanted to gather myself and find a starting point for what comes next, to breathe.

I'm worn in the middle
neither a shape

nor its shadow   as a drawn string
in this willing garden

trembles at the touch
of one I've never met

she turns a peg
my heart

tightens slightly
but this is her own

concerto of everything
an avenue of sorrows

sublime and rough
as a road can be

COLUMBUS TO PEEBLES, AND THE GREAT SERPENT MOUND
third day

I just passed Chillicothe and a town called Deadman Crossing. The sway of the road with its forks and turns feels like a movie about the love of a car. Desiccated cornfields wait for harvest in the papery light. The crop has been planted right up to the houses where a bare patch of treeless yard leaves nothing to interrupt the coming extraction. A car speeds by every few minutes. There are only a couple of feet of shoulder on which to pull off, as if even that would use too much land. The only place with a bit of nature is a triangle of sunken ground where two roads meet.

in a corner the sprayer
can't reach, a refugium of asters,
coneflowers dialing the sun, their feet
in the last dark place they can go

A Penobscot story says that Corn Mother was also First Mother, who gave up her body to feed her starving people. She tells her husband, "Let two of our sons take hold of my hair and drag me back and forth, back and forth, over every patch until my flesh has been torn from my body." Her husband seeks guidance from the Great Instructor, his uncle Kloskurbeh, and they follow her instructions. Nothing happens for weeks, but then her flesh turns into corn and her buried bones become the tobacco plant with its gift of smoke.[3] The book where this is found calls it a legend. To the Penobscot it would have been a sacred story. The difference is everything.

a child grows up with a story
what is required, maybe of her,

so she enters the blood of it
passes it on

I turn near the outskirts of Peebles and head seven miles north. The park road winds upward through scrub and young trees that mask the forest of oak and white ash behind them. The Serpent Mound is an earthen effigy that loops for over 1,300 feet. The hilltop was used by different peoples. Dates range from the Adena people about 300 BCE to Fort Ancient culture, 1,100 years ago.[4] The winding body points toward a cliff overlooking Bush Creek. The head points to the summer solstice sunset. The creature's open mouth appears to be swallowing an egg, which is all that remains of a mound that was probably an altar.

A brother and sister, who can't be more than six, squeal as they roll down a grassy cone of earth next to the parking lot. Their exhausted mother sits at the picnic table, slouching slightly and smoking a cigarette. It isn't clear if she saw the warning sign; the kids are climbing an Adena burial mound. It once held the remains of a six-foot man. The body was laid on a bed of hot ash and covered with clay. He must have been important. Nine shallow graves known as intrusions were added to the sides and top later. I head for the rickety-looking steel lookout tower at the tail of the serpent. The edge of the narrow plateau looks over treetops that follow the dangerous drop to the creek. The fringe has been cleared and seeded with grass. But this is not wrong. It would have looked like this a thousand years ago with shadows locked in the coils, tracing the body that could be seen from hilltops miles away. I love the otherness and the archaeology of the place, but I am here for something else.

in the coil and the hour
in the parking lot of Things That Fall Away and my
Perpetual Commitment to Nothing
the voice in my head lifts hello
to these present dead—spirits
beneath this legal lawn
a line I didn't think a person like me
could cross

~~~

It doesn't matter what you've done, or where you come from. Here at the FHMCC, everyone is welcomed with open arms. Our community is warm and inviting. We simply want to "love the Hell outta ya..."[5]
~~~

on 13 Harleys
disciples of the First Heavy Metal Church of Christ
roll up to the washroom   these aren't the leggy
brunette not-quite-biker chicks in Day of the Dead face paint
on the FHMCC website
they're more like the paunchy
grandparents of said girls though one or two
could have done a stretch
in Chillicothe pen before these
God's Dirt
Prayer Warrior badges
and seventeen hundred and fifty CCs of thundering
Harley-Davidson saved them

one of the wives says to the other *I think*
it's some kind of mound or something
her husband limps thirty feet behind
because there comes a time when a sixty-year-old body
doesn't need this shit

Where are we going now? the first wife says
I don't know   says the other
and keeps walking

~~~

head to tail thirteen hundred feet
of serpent loops to the whirr and click
of electric wheelchairs
Is it *vemonous*? a kid asks his mom

the snake likes the heat   the stripes
left by the mower   the slant
of the path and a thousand
years to savour the egg a
bout to slide into its mouth

~~~

anima or *animus* some shadows are made
of morning   and some of the evening

they never meet in this world
though they've heard of each other

or believe there are others like them
it must be so   people do the same thing

~~~

eyes at my age can no longer
take the setting sun

no tours now just two women coming up
from Bush Creek trail   and We-wä'-see   *Shawnee for vulture*
checking her clan
she's getting to know me

the Adena mound is wrapped
in the magic hour

I circle the base which takes
longer than I thought

what can I say to a spirit's repose
it's not the language

that matters
so I say   Tansi   *a greeting in Cree*
~~~

I circle the grave again
Brother tansi

maybe this is not right but it feels
like a ceremony to me

A TOWN CALLED LEBANON

evening, third day

The light is fading. I decide to carry on to Fort Ancient. The Hopewell built the three-and-a-half-mile earthen wall that follows a ridge cut deeper by the Little Miami River 270 feet below it. The seventy gateways of the so-called Fort would have been useless for defence. The wall rises twenty-three feet at the highest point and encloses two large gathering spaces connected by a thin neck of land like an hourglass. The map tries to join them. The museum is closed, but at least I have my bearings. I need to find a motel, so I head for Lebanon, a small city at the end of a chain of places I've passed since this morning—Belfast, Washington Township, and Licking County named for its natural salts that attract deer. I think of a friend who carefully slices the place names from wall maps with an X-ACTO blade. The spaces left by the cuts cluster like paragraphs of code without a key. The contour lines of old mountains, alpine meadows, and valley bottoms have been filled in with a matte green wash. The shading stops for a river with its settler name removed.

Fort Ancient
is no fort at all

the Little Miami   a river
far from any sea

I pull off in a town called Lebanon
Knights Inn   50 dollars a knight

behind Taco Bell on East Main   Google shows Mound Street
Mound Crescent   then HWY 48 dead-ends

Chillicothe Avenue is Shawnee at least
(though not the Avenue part)

tired as I am I have to laugh   it's easier
to shred a map than a name

FORT ANCIENT
morning, fourth day

I take my time on my way back to Fort Ancient. I cross the Miami and pull over to look back from the far side of the bridge. The Little Miami is a designated Wild and Scenic River that drops down from the woodlands and farms of five counties. The river begins as a nondescript stream, then descends 111 miles through gorges and pools connected by short sections of faster water until it finally joins the Ohio. I follow the path others have made from the bridge to a patch of stony shore. Deep treed slopes catch the heat as mid-morning light baffles the water. Ripples form and roll, riding the current in slow motion as they join other lines, the edges of smooth sheets of water that break apart and trail past me. I think of the rivers back home, their silty bottoms and tear-shaped sandbars building up grain by grain on one side and losing on the other. If I followed the Miami's peaceable course, I would see a different country—a fragile wholeness that's easily loved and just as easily shed. The river's like a voice that wants me to follow it to its source, to take a day and head north, but I have to keep moving. My heart will have to catch up.

we are the animal
drawn to water, drawn also
to regret

The museum lawn is packed with cars. I have turned up in the middle of a triathlon. I'm directed down a row of cars parked on the grass. Cyclists pull up to the tents, weaving between clumps of waiting families and the race marshals. Inside the museum, the iron tools and nineteenth-century maps meant to illuminate the narrative of settlement are oddly familiar. I've seen them most of my life. I watch ten minutes of a film on the three miles of wall that are still mostly a mystery. The narration is familiar, so I head outside for the actual place and the southern field. The grassy opening is much larger than I imagined—at least ten acres encircled by trees that the builders would have pushed back farther. It feels free, its own place except for the occasional voice of a hiker on a trail I can't see. The sign on a waist-high post marks the footpath into the trees. It splits to the right along a finger of land to a lookout point. The undulating canopy below hides the Little

Miami as it threads its way westward and vanishes into the distant hills. The Fort Ancient wall is camouflaged by undulating woodland and scattered trees. In Fort Ancient times, the land would have been cleared to observe the seasons, the sun and moon, and to the north, the stars turning counter-clockwise across the valley's bowl. The gaps in the wall connect to each other in a series of airy hyphens in a language only the builders could read.

starlit swale
on a page made of earth

if not for night
we would know nothing

The triathlon is over. I take a seat in front of the small, makeshift stage where a greying rock band lampoons the president before an evaporating audience of relatives and friends. I'm certain I've missed something important. On my way to the car, I walk by a low, nondescript mound covered by a layer of flat stones. It looks like students working for the park dumped it here or maybe it's some minor remnant. It doesn't take long to discover my mistake. Four of these mounds form a perfect square 512 feet on each side. Huge ceremonial fires were built on top of them turning the original limestone red and crumbly, and the fossils white. These are calendar stones. A sightline from this one leads to a gate for observing the summer solstice. Other lines point to the major lunar standstill and to the minor standstill 9.3 years later. I cross the lawn and the highway that brought me here last night to the gap where the solstice sun rises.

at the Fort Ancient wall
who is walking   I am walking

in whose lifetime
this is my lifetime

what happened to this stone
this stone is burnt

what burned it
belief burned it

I trace the solstice line back to the calendar mound. I go into the museum and buy a DVD and two ready-to-assemble corn dolls. The maker was a woman for sure, maybe Shawnee. I'm not that far south, but night here falls earlier than I'm used to. I don't want to be driving in darkness in a place I don't know. I'll take the shortest way back to Columbus.

COLUMBUS
fifth day

All I want to do is have my first decent breakfast in days and get centred. I take a window table of the Brioso Café with my copy of the *Columbus Dispatch*. There's a headline about a shooting on the front page but I don't want to read it. America loves its disasters. I finish my coffee and *huevos*, then head to the Columbus Metropolitan Library. There must be a hundred people working on laptops or cell phones—seniors, young people looking up jobs or apartments, and grad students getting ready for seminars. Some are here for the free Wi-Fi. I like the *click* and *hum* of it. I settle in facing the floor-to-ceiling window filled by a park and the white twenty-one-storey office tower next door.

American flags have been fluttering over the lines of colonial porches in the small towns I've been driving though all week. A few have yellow ribbons for a son or daughter or spouse in the military overseas. The real thing says more than that Tony Orlando "Yellow Ribbon" song ever did—a song for another war. The US flag on top of the insurance building next to the library droops against the pole. It looks like the flag's at half-mast. At first, I think a soldier from here has died in Iraq. Yesterday was October 1. While I was making my way home last night, a gunman was firing 1,100 rounds into a crowd at a music festival in Las Vegas. No one I've met has said anything about it.

Guns in so many houses. Over
the Motorists Insurance Building, the first
flag I've seen today, half-mast
and failing. Me with no TV
thinking *Iraq*.

I skipped the *Dispatch*'s
front page, "Shooter in Vegas." Didn't
like that so I turned to Page 3.
Two death penalties, a notice
of appeals, retrial denied.
Why ask a killer who wants
to live after all, or the aproned
young man stirring my latte in

the library café as light
floods the books: what's left
when coverage teaches
the next person how? It's hard
to decode the silence.
Murder. The new norm.

RAIN DAY ONE

Morning rain comes and goes. October heat leaves everything breathless. The library's limestone façade stores the heat like everything else. Patrons cluster around the shaded patio tables outside. Trees in the seven-acre topiary park have been pruned to mimic precisely the bathers, people with umbrellas and strollers, the dogs, ducks, and even the contours of Georges Seurat's huge impressionist painting, *A Sunday Afternoon on the Island of La Grande Jatte*. A pair of cyclists in stylish jerseys and black, close-fitting shorts and families looking for a wisp of air on the walkway are part of the scheme. I need the routine, the pause that the rain has forced me into. It has been a long time since I've had time to think of Isle of Lewis, of Callanish and the path between the stones that brought me here.

I wasn't attached
to a word like *glyph*
felt sorry
for the girl playing cello on a freezing patio
rubbing her hands to keep her fingers from getting stiff
the ground quite stony

and the wind indifferent
I thought
polestar
wrote *headland*
all that holy diction of latitude and declination   spirals
talking among themselves
the huge machinery of stars
                    almost casual

RAIN DAY TWO

Work in my room. Desk moved to the window, view of three or four rooftops, the suggestion of a neighbourhood and a few feet of yard.

I worry
about things I'm not seeing   purple finch

on the power line   a small
ordinary moon with a beak

the book of *Origins* says   on islands or hilltops
small things become more like themselves

like this story
memory bends

RAIN DAY THREE

I've been trying to make contact with the Native American Indian Center of Central Ohio. I couldn't find an email, and state directory information service says they don't have the number. Maybe they're all using cells. My time's running out and I want to at least make contact. So I just hopped in the car and came. I'll come back later if they're busy. I want to let them know I'm here and perhaps even take in an event. There's no sign on the door and the office is locked. They could be in meetings or dealing with a crisis, and have no time for what a Cree friend would call an *omantewak*, a guest passing through. I wait in my car on the narrow street. I'd be suspicious of me if I lived here. I don't feel safe, or maybe it's just that I've come unannounced like some tourist, a *flâneur* who's done nothing for them. But it's just a first try.

The thunder I've been hearing is getting closer—a low amplitude vibration like a large stack of lumber being moved around, then suddenly dropped. I have to get back to my B&B before the rain hits. I'll pick up a burger and eat in my room. Regardless of the weather, my time is running out. Rain or shine, I have to get to the Great Circle at Heath tomorrow. There's not much to say about today's non-event. I'll be glad to get out of the city.

> The pages won't stay in their piles. I can't keep
> the scenes straight. It's clear I've come to an edge
> a place with no barrier, where fools walk out
> on the ledge that's crumbling beneath them. It's not
> a big deal, then you look down facing the arrogance
> that delivered you here. A stiffening breeze
> could sweep you away, and everyone watching
> would simply say, well there goes a fool
> and head back to their cars.

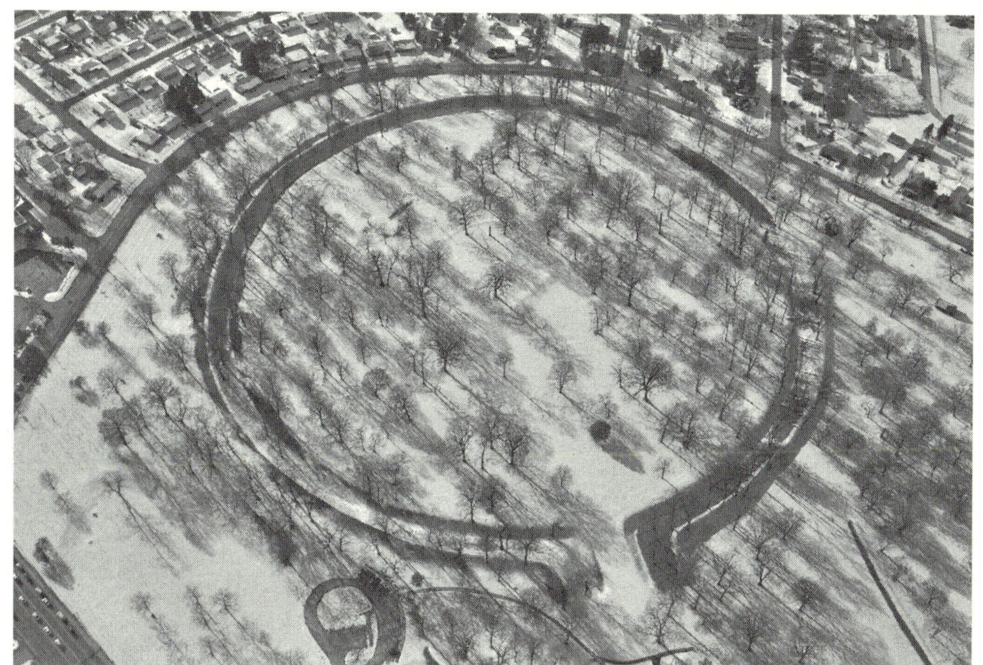

Great Circle in winter, Heath, Ohio. The dark area inside the wall is a channel that once held water, perhaps to guide spirits into the circle.

Timothy E. Black/Newark Earthworks Center. Reproduced with permission.

THE GREAT CIRCLE, HEATH, OH
ninth day

The prairie horizon I trusted is gone. My half-finished breakfast wrap sits on the passenger seat. It's been all GPS and directional media since I landed. I feel I've woken up at a great distance from where I went to sleep. I got up early and have driven to Heath forty-five minutes away. I turn off at the ramp. The post and beam strip malls, an appliance store, and other businesses are casually spread. The real town heart is somewhere else. I nearly miss the low blue sign on Hebron Road that says simply, "Great Circle Earthworks, Greater Licking County." I expected something more to bring in tourists, but anonymity is a way some places have of saving what's left.

The parking lot is empty except for two women pulling rain jackets from their car. I look up at the lee slope of a hill sprinkled with tall, volunteer trees. The ground between them has been groomed, making it hard to tell where the natural slope becomes the arc of a massive wall, a curving trajectory that disappears into the pewter sky. The Circle wall encloses twenty acres. It follows the contours of the hilltop, rising fourteen feet in places to make a level horizon of the rim. A carefully groomed channel follows the inside circumference. It used to hold water, perhaps to guide spirits into the Circle. The ditch is dry now, giving the illusion that the wall is even higher than it was when it still held the ring of water that would have reflected the sky.

> the brochure said
> a man-built ring   diameter
>
> 1,052 feet   circumference
> two feet from perfect
>
> think eyelid   or henge
> not how you got here

Using fire, hand tools, and baskets to move the earth, the Hopewell levelled the hilltop overlooking the Scioto River. After the burn, wild grasses and flowers would have received the rain just as the seeded grass does now. My shoes are soaked. The entrance is the gap where the two ends of the

Circle slope down to ground, leaving a space which is the only way into the centre. Snatches of white-sided bungalows on Parkview Drive blink over the rim of the far wall. Maybe they're here for the commute to Columbus, maybe for privacy and a place to run the dog. But there are other parks and no algorithm to explain what brought them to this particular place and its boundary. I hesitate. A few steps ahead, I'm surprised by a group of eighty-foot red maples I couldn't see from the entrance. A fallen main limb has been dragged into the open to be cleared off. The storm that did it must have been recent. I choose a direction and start walking.

last night's rain not quite
turning to steam

a tree has fallen   its skin
warm like an elephant's

still-moist cambium where the bark's
split away   cooler

than the grey-wrapped limb
as if the sap knew something was up

a tree has fallen

I'm only halfway to the far wall. There's a dark spot at the base. I imagine a pile of fieldstones, maybe a hearth. All I find is the trunk of a tree sheared flat by a chainsaw, the heartwood turned black by the rot that killed it. A pearl crescent butterfly flashes the small half-moons on its wingtips as it catches a bit of heat, a current I can't quite feel. I think of the Hopi butterfly dance painting in the Columbus Museum, questions of figure and ground, white paint on white paper except for the black lustre of the young girl's hair and painted triangle mask. The maiden has learned the thirty-two songs of the ceremony. She has no word for time.

her gaze is direct
butterfly dance
butterfly wing powder

more and more
intimate things of the world put in drawers
or in rooms' dim light to keep them from fading

Something above me yips like a terrier. A harassing squirrel? Scolding bird? Eventually the bird flies off, becomes its own silhouette on the short, quick route to another tree. On which, a pictogram.

delinquents in love carve

this ♥'s Trevor
beside one ♥ (indecipherable)

a small ♥
Renno Lisa Javon
proudly indicates ↗
for ZACK B.G. who is taller

but why in 20 acres four lovers
a single tree hard to find for anyone but them

A maple in full autumn colour stands by itself, crimson in its own forest. Back home, the only trees like this were in books. I lived on the pine tree line where spruce grew so thick they blocked everything but the riverhead of stars directly above us. The moon came out in its own time. There was no place like this. The red I see here I can love, not the legend of a colour valorized in rhyming poems in cinder block schools. Still, we loved those famous Group of Seven painters of the North. Teachers called it *our* North—Precambrian, scraped, ghost-skinned birches gripped to a stony point in a forest not yet subdued. In classroom posters: Tom Thompson's silent canoe, A.Y. Jackson, Frank Carmichael—and blue-green swirling, Emily Carr's Mister Woo, our favourite monkey, perched on the paint cart confirming *This is the colour. The world looks like this.*

Painters pass. It's the next generation's work to break free of them. But I still love those smoke-green vales I saw in my mind, a garden's fall and tangle, autumn proclaimed as the freezing rush of a stream past a screen of saplings.

Ice
and fire
the carmine wilderness they said was true really *was* true—this one colour
I never got to see until now. Fifty years later, in another country.

REMEMBERING AND FORGETTING

late afternoon, ninth day, in Columbus

Every city has its theory of streets, its stops and flows, a diction I'm getting to know. I'm glad to be back in Columbus, heading to Ohio State University for a lecture by Robin Fleming, a visiting professor from Boston College. The classroom is subterranean, a dressed-up space in the basement of the library. The title is a little macabre, "Remembering (and Forgetting) Little Corpses in Late Roman and Early Medieval Britain." I'm surprised to find a hundred chairs set in neat rows across the length of the room are mostly taken. The notice turned up on an OSU Events email a friend sent me. The subject is arcane, but it started me thinking about the burial of children, who are rarely mentioned in the Earthworks literature. Fleming is talking about material culture in Britain—the messages left in skeletal remains and daily objects as the Roman Empire fell apart.

in the long rooms of history
the body
the slag

stones in a high place
look for a barrow
under a field look for the floor

The absence of children in these late Roman period cemeteries led some to think that child mortality rates were so high that the deaths of children of commoners were not given a high importance. Scholars said the missing children's graves might be a sign of parental detachment due to the high emotional cost of investing in a child who would likely die. It has even been said that the absence of children could be evidence of a common practice of infanticide. It's an appalling theory. The simpler explanation turns out to be quite moving.[6] Most low-status people weren't buried in cemeteries. Children were buried under the floors of their families' homes. The earliest graves were covered by stone slabs, and then the house was built over them. The small bodies were accompanied by dogs, pets, coins, and even whole birds. Some had shoes, which may be associated with the winged sandals of Mercury. The pits were large enough for an adult to get in to arrange the tableau. And if Roman, perhaps they said what a grieving father left on his daughter's stone,

> *sit tibi terra levis* / may the earth
> lie lightly upon you

The slides remind me of the children here, laid to rest in small, elusive settlements yet to be found, not with the finery of important persons but with the familiar things of their lives: favourite bracelets, shell ornaments, and gestures of devotion.

> that tenderness
> of things in ourselves we can't take apart

From my grandparents' generation to mine, those same children would have gone into the Indian residential school system. How different those endings were. A child's odds of death in a residential school were the same as a Canadian soldier's in World War II. Thousands lie in unmarked graves. Often, parents weren't notified. No matter how much of the covering narrative we have begun to strip away, my own generation has yet to face the truth of it.

My father taught at the Beauval Indian Residential School in northwest Saskatchewan after the Meadow Lake Tribal Council took it over. I drove six hours to meet him and stayed in his rustic cabin by Lac La Plonge. He must have seemed eccentric to his fellow teachers living in town.

> the north
> forest-present, heading toward the legend
> of who he was

> who I was
> better than him, he was hoping
> and it made him feel free

I read poems to his class and answered their questions. When I was done, I found the student who had been watching me warily. He hardly said a word, but after a sentence or two he shoved a thick stack of poems toward me. It was almost a dare and I liked that. It's still a good memory. But Beauval also had a graveyard beside it. A fire broke out in the convent in 1927. It killed nineteen boys between seven and twelve years of age, and one teacher. The worn markers were small and featureless except for the names. They seemed to be bought as cheaply as possible, as if there were a warehouse full of them somewhere. I walked the rows where the children lay buried together. Even that modest eloquence was stained by the fact there were other children's graves that had nothing to do with the fire. More recently, knowledge keepers and sacred pipe keepers held a clearing ceremony to help the spirits of these children move on.

In Regina, where I live, there are at least thirty-eight unmarked graves in the cemetery of the former Regina Indian Industrial School (RIIS). This is not an unusual number and there could be more. It was common practice to bury multiple bodies in a single grave. It's a 680-square-metre piece of farmland next to Pinkie Road, a dusty grid road used by heavy trucks west of the city. It's still not easy to find—a square island of ground that rises slightly from the wheat field on three sides. The coyotes, jack rabbits, and birds gathering seeds in a few tough patches of dusty scrub seem true to the small lives that rest close by. The first time I went there I walked carefully. Survivors of these schools, their children and families, had been there before me. They left plush animal toys on the edge of the small clumps of bush. Others tied carefully wrapped gifts of tobacco to the tips of the branches. Even the emptiness has a weight. The writer Lee Maracle (Stó:lō First Nation) said, "The dead miss us too." I visit the cemetery each spring after the snow clears and then through the summer. I straighten a few things up as respectfully as I can and think my own thoughts.

Start at age 60
subtract 14 years, when RIIS got them
times 38 children buried, no plaque
1748 years   life lost [7]

How different First Nation burials are from what happened in Beauval and west of Regina. Not long ago, I attended the funeral of a friend's grandson in a First Nation community in the Qu'Appelle Valley. The valley is the rich, mile-wide bed of a glacial river that drops down from a rim of original prairie. Noah was born premature and never made it home except to be buried.[8] A sacred fire was kept burning through the night until the ceremony was done the next day. Forty people turned up. They did everything themselves. They had a tradition of buying two new shovels to make the grave. As we gathered around, a group of drummers sang "You Are My Sunshine"—the principal voice of the drum, the drummers' high, wavering voices, and the song I thought I knew transfixing me there. The men filled the rectangular scar in the frozen ground. My friend took a shovel; then his son, the father, passed one to me. I worked silently, then passed it on after what felt like a respectful time.

From my back-row seat in the OSU Library, I think of the small magic of all the resting places I walked past this week without knowing. I think of carved birds, bracelets gently laid, and the care that went into them, and of Noah:

LITTLE SUN BEAR

born in the month when young bears
are born. His father, his uncles say nothing as they pass
two new shovels between them and fill in the grave.

No one speaks on this cold sunny day at the end
of the lake. The ice on the old road melts. Aunties weep,
uncles take turns until the job's done.

The Elder's a sun dancer who says
the white bear from the north
frightens Summer away.

"The sun doesn't sink, it *falls,* in our language," he says.
When he was young, he pierced himself, then danced
for two days to honor the Creator,

twelve poles raised, he said, *like apostles*
as he fasted under the arbor: this story
for Noah.

Circles then. Directions.
Needle and thread grass
to cover his grave in spring.*

---

* NOTE TO THE READER: Noah's story and poem are shared here with permission of the family.

ON THE GREAT HOPEWELL ROAD

From 1820 on, early amateur archaeologists, surveyors, and writers have reported walls and fragments of an ancient Hopewell Road possibly linking the Newark Earthworks to the Chillicothe area, sixty miles to the southwest—the location of Mound City, with other sites along the way. The Hopewell Road's existence over the whole distance has not been proven conclusively, but the accumulated research, including satellite imaging and studies of the topography, make it a possibility that's still being studied. The confirmed portions predate the Mayan and Anasazi sacred roads and pathways to their places of pilgrimage and ceremony. In 1862, James and Charles Salisbury traced a six-mile section that passed between baked clay walls that were much different from the earth they rested on. Urban spawl, development, and agriculture have left gaps in the known parts of the road today. A 2008 LIDAR study by Romaine and Burks used pulses of laser light to measure terraine features. They measured a 150-foot distance between the two walls. The remains were only a foot high. In other places, changes in the soil were all that could be found where the road had been.[9]

As with other corridors in the Earthworks... it was walked in a sacred way different and separate from everyday footpaths. Walking the road, these ancient pilgrims rendered the three-dimensional map into themselves, embodying the map by inhabiting it.

—MARGARET WICKENS PEARCE (Potawatomi)[10]

FROM TRIP ADVISOR, WITH THREE REVIEWS

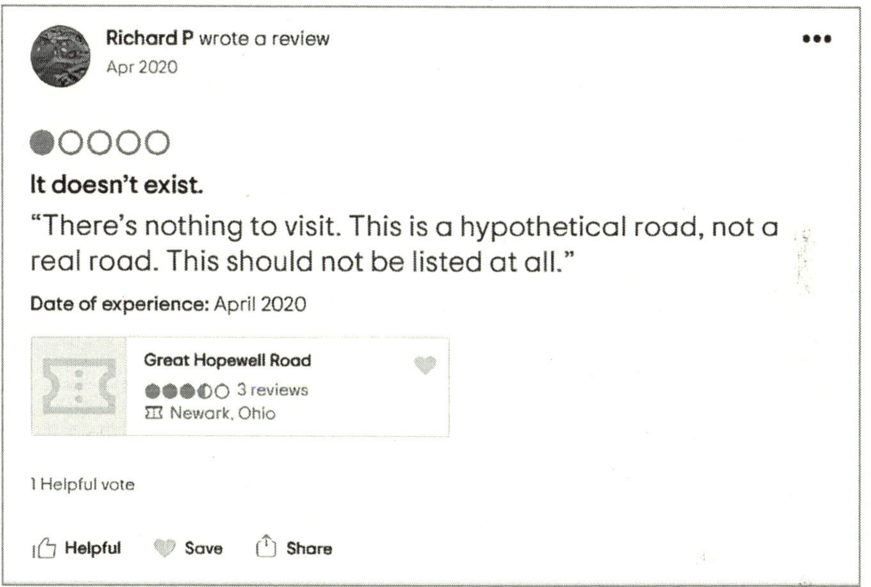

THE GREAT HOPEWELL ROAD:
GIS SOLUTIONS TOWARD PATHWAY DISCOVERY

Found text excerpts, study by Timothy A. Price [11]

Introduction

Connect these works for they contain

circular and

octagonal arrangements aligned in
ritual

we can begin to examine
where to locate just such a road

Methodology

Known places were obtained

lineation
flat ground

cover types the road would have been located near rivers

earthworks
the possibility of landscape

Discussion

the projected calculations are likely
extraneous

look solely at
the earth

the model falls the entire model falls

Results

Slope and land intimate
familiarity

upon closer examination "events" occur
looking at becomes

indeed a hotbed

MOUND CITY, CHILLICOTHE, OH
eleventh day

Mound City is a rectangular enclosure with twenty-three burial mounds, where the bones and remains of important people were brought to be cremated. The ceremonies were held under wooden structures that were removed later and the mounds built over them. One of the artifacts is an eleven-by-seven-inch effigy of a human hand. The hand is delicately carved from a translucent sheet of mica from North Carolina.

next to the ash bed   palm
and fingers upheld

a hand
blue and amber
comes forth from the dark in a sign
even you can read

                    you may come this far
          and no farther
says the one
                                        who still owns it

I stop to pick up a brochure with a small map of the grounds at the Visitor Center. I tell the park officer I'm a writer from Canada. We talk about where I've been so far. She says I should follow the edge of the compound to the place on the Scioto River believed to be a landing for boats bearing the dead. It's the river that speaks to her. She hardly mentions the mounds. I leave the centre and turn south across the enclosure. The overgrown boundary I saw from a distance becomes indecipherable where it merges with the encroaching forest. I find the worn concrete steps that descend to a walkway above the Scioto. The treacherous bank falls four body lengths to scoured black rocks and the river. I have to stop myself from pitching forward as I'm startled by the ripping of leaves and the gunshot-crack of a shagbark hickory nut's hundred-foot fall to the ground. Where I grew up, trees don't do this; even a slight snap is never a good sound to hear in the bush behind you. The trees here grow straight and taller than anything on the open prairie. I love the music of the genus *Carya.*

Black Walnut / Butternut / Bitternut
Shagbark / Shellbark.

In forests I know
the four o'clock wind
is dropping, but this wind ruffles

once until dusk
boats arriving
bones of the dead delivered in baskets, pots
of ashes, the desiccated bodies still loved.

The Scioto readies itself
leaves wheel over the river's drift
this one rises, holds its breath
as I time the return, twenty-eight seconds
over the water
then the voice in my head says

I am the messenger who has no message.
You need to stop looking.

Mound City. Strange name for a place where no city was. The word *grave* isn't right for those brought to lie here in clear sight of the lean, autumn sky. The park is closing. I want to find the mound that should be close by. It doesn't take much for a burial in a wood to be missing. I look for the slight undulation or change in the plant cover that might lead me to it. I check my watch and give up. A family of crows lifts up from their branches. Three of them take turns leading me as I make my way back. I make that crow sound from the back of my throat, a trick I've known since I was a kid. One of them answers. Their nests are easy to find in the bare autumn trees. I have visited the dead; I have visited the river. These noisy companions who watch what I do remind me of home. They have their ways and we both know it. *A disappearing grave,* they say in their dry voices. *Cousin, we're joking you.*

THE MOUNDBUILDERS COUNTRY CLUB, SITE OF THE OCTAGON AND OBSERVATORY CIRCLE

Sunday afternoon, twelfth day, Newark, OH

This is the last of four days each year when the public is allowed to walk the grounds of the golf course built over the site known as the Octagon and Observatory Circle. The two perfectly aligned forms are part of a four-square-mile complex that includes the largest set of geometric earthen enclosures in the world. The Moundbuilders Country Club has opened the grounds to displays set up by Ohio History Connection, small clusters of tourists, local couples, and history buffs. We drift over the course and stay off the greens.

> *The fourth hole is named "the Veldt"...One must maintain a straight course or the mound on one side and the gully on the other will play havoc with his score. When encountering a spirit or ghost, let him play through.*
>
> —*Newark Advocate* in a caution to the golfer, 1911[12]

The Octagon alone covers fifty acres. Twenty-five Stonehenges would fit inside it. There are six earthen walls 550 feet long and two shorter ones. A broad path between two more walls connects the Octagon to Observatory Circle, which encloses another twenty acres. A smaller circle off to the side that was probably used for communal gatherings has been converted to an immaculate green for one of the links. The original arrangement with the Club, which leases the site, may have saved it from being lost like so many of its sister sites, but it would be an understatement to call the arrangement an anachronism in this day and age.[13]

Simply by being here I feel two conflicting narratives. In one, I am here because of the resonance I felt among the stones of Callanish, near my own people's home. We carry the code of our ancestors' places inside us. Not just the stories in a grandchild's mind, but the rock or plain or sea we came from—the lives and deaths that brought us to who we are. We're earthed in scenes we know before we ever see the actual place, where fields too rocky to be ploughed, heights of land, and the half-buried stones too heavy to be moved already know us.

Like the builders on Isle of Lewis, the Hopewell must have intended to evoke a direct experience of the sacred, to open the mind to a different story of the world and how we got here. Our own smallness is part of it. One writer says our response and sense of connection to a site like this is a form of conservation of the place itself. The avenues and open spaces, the Great Circle at Heath, or the lines one walks here don't feel ancient. Despite the size, it feels like an intimate conversation with strangers who never left.

In the second version, I am part of a certain class of cultural tourist, the kind visitor bureaus like to talk about—hotel patrons who leave their dollars in restaurants and casinos, and whose travel stories told in neighbouring states and abroad validate the enterprise and its contradictions.

my airfare
lodging and rented car
a wringing of hands
that comes from too much
money or not enough

Our guide, Tim Jordan,[14] qualifies much of what he says. This must be the archaeologist in him, patient and methodical. Or perhaps he believes Keats, the poet who said the point of the mystery is not knowing. The Circle and Octagon are aligned so that standing on the crest of Observatory Mound, one can watch the standstill moonrise from the opening on the far side of the Octagon, almost three thousand feet away. The line is half a degree from perfect.

The Hopewell used what is known as the angle of repose. This is the angle that sand or similar material will form on its own. It is the most stable angle for an earthwork and the reason these walls retain their shape after two thousand years. Grass helps to keep their integrity intact. A visiting architect said the builders probably knew more about this kind of construction than we do today.

the angle of repose
our lives and how things settle
belief
and the covering
that keeps it all in

There must have been a great ceremonial purpose behind the 18.6-year lunar cycle in the design. The standstill itself could have had no agricultural or other practical purpose. Jordan works at Flint Ridge Memorial State Park, which includes an eight-mile-long seam of flint, which is technically called chert. The colour changes dramatically when the material is heated to make flaking easier. It includes streaks of red and dusty rose and a range of yellows and blues that are even more stunning when held up to the light.

when rock is broken apart
with a purpose

there's a crack like a grave being opened
and a time as it's turned

the angle judged in the left hand
and the place to strike

Woodland Cree tell
that a being chased almost to death

hid in a stone
and was trapped there

when I consider in museums
these bits of the world   heated

                hafted
sharp flakes

falling like blossoms of fire
I think I believe it

Back at the display tents, I introduce myself to Marti Chaatsmith (Comanche/Choctaw), who is the associate director of the Newark Earthworks Center. She told me about today's tour in an email. She's the only Indigenous person I've met all week. We speak briefly, but I don't want to presume too much and other people need to speak to her. Marti suggests that I follow the edge of the Circle to Raccoon Creek. There is always water at these places.

walk
circumspectly

bent grass green
fairways at rest

four days a year
the place is itself

silt trapped by algae
turns the creek bed brown

rain wakes
the beauty beneath

just as the moon

shines brightly or dimly
on the plain that contains it

Archaeology these days is full of regression models, data points, and infrared imagery. I used to study maps in my job. They were usually part of a technique called triangulation, a way to know the shape of a thing from its outside points. You look at the physical place and the way people see it in their mind. You add data and maps and make a frame from the stories. The gaps are important. This feels like what I'm doing now. I double back across the Octagon and join a group halfway through the second tour. I recognize our guide, Brad Lepper, from what he has written about the way these geometries connect. The theory is that this site is part of a great ceremonial machine of world renewal, with the rituals associated with the honoured dead as its engine.[15] Others speak of "a grand unity of Earth, Sky and Mind."[16] The open space is a commons where people could participate directly in the cosmic rhythms. The imagination behind it must have been extraordinary.

But our guide keeps it light. He knows who we are: the man beside me who talks about his private collection of Native American pieces, his wife, a few tourists, and a couple of locals. We pass between the pair of walls I take for a ceremonial way linking the Octagon to the Circle. We agree not to speak. Swallows criss-cross the space over our heads as they wheel after insects.

nothing to say   our voices
                        sink into walls without coming back
            the walls see it
the standstill moon behind us like a kind of proof

Our little group crosses the open ground. Observatory Mound is a 170-foot-long earthen form that looks back over the whole site and pulls the ends of the Circle in behind it. The early Hopewell filled in the resulting passage through the mound into the heart of the Circle. No one knows why. I follow two women and an older couple to the top of the mound. A few years from now, the standstill moon will rise from the gate at the end of the Octagon more than half a mile away. I walk the spine of the mound the way we walk a dugout berm back home—scanning the fields for coyotes, deer, or maybe a pair of antelope as the horizon tips downward at the ends. I've been scratching in notebooks for twelve days. Small things encountered by accident speak to me because they are *my* accidents while discoveries that take pages to describe are lost in the scale of the actual place. There are so many gates—eight entrances to the Octagon, the gate for the Circle here and its sister Great Circle at Heath, and seventy more at Fort Ancient. *Gate* may not even be the right word for it, and certainly not one the builders used. I consider staying longer to go through them all—listening and watching at each one with what a friend calls "attention," a way of being in a place on its own terms, to suspend the chatter of one's self. But that would take weeks. A walk through the long-forgotten gate behind me will have to do. When I get there, I realize it isn't a gate anymore. Weeds and thorny scrub have made it their own. The path that should have been here is closed in by thick bush and woodland. I've been in forests before, dense ones. There's a kind of warning anxiety a person gets just before losing a sense of direction. These woods aren't like that. Still, the wildness that used to be here feels close, the waist-high tangle blocks every step. I don't think it wants me.

COLUMBUS MUSEUM OF ART
Last day

Somewhere along the line I think I've contracted the pilgrim's addiction to epiphany. I've spent everything. My suitcase is safe in the car, my GPS device is back in its box. The museum's a quiet place to spend the last few hours before my flight home. The sign in the foyer draws me to a group of digital portraits made from the reflected light of oils by Velázquez, Rembrandt, and Van Dyck. I'm just another white-haired customer on a bench in one of those paintings in which the subject disappears. Pliny the Elder thought that light comes from our eyes, striking objects in the dark world where it's reflected back to us, making things visible in a kind of continuous archaeology of the present. Perhaps he was right.

The word *standstill* wasn't even in my mind when I put my hand on that glyph at Callanish. I didn't know what it meant. Even so, I felt the memory stir, that part of myself I could only meet by being there. It's here too. That, and what a subtle thing the ground we walk over so easily is. The Hopewell knew it well. No one uses the word *monument* for what is still alive here, the gate the moon uses and what it renews as the century gets more and more difficult.

faith grows thinner as a small screen erases
what fell inside us   the reason

the builders used earth
which is stronger than stone

The debate isn't over. It took years to notice the standstill alignments at Callanish and Stenness in Scotland, at Chimney Rock, the Light Dagger at Fajada Butte, and along these rivers—the Scioto, the Little Miami, Bush Creek, and Raccoon Creek. We try to frame the mystery even as we doubt the science that built it. Unlike the marble temples of antiquity, these spaces were made for the human scale. Nothing resists. They invite the human gaze: the view of the heavens, eye-level walls with grass growing over them, the cleared plateaus, sightlines and gates, and the way to the river, dusty asters, maples illuminated in their autumn halos, beech trees and butterfly weed, native grasses, and my friends the crows. In the days of the Hopewell, the surrounding forest was home. It provided a healthy diet of nuts, game, forest food, and produce they grew in small gardens. They must have had an intimate familiarity with the very earth they built with and everything here.

The Hopewell dead show no signs of battle. What they built was the result of a remarkable collectivity that lasted five hundred years. Crossing the Great Circle at Heath or walking through gates as anyone can, I'm not as overwhelmed as I might have been. There's a sense of anticipation, the patient, pervasive kind that waits in a clearing or newly mown field for something yet to come. Two thousand years after the fact the standstill will come with or without us. These gates will mark it as they always have.

I leave as I came   by a map
made of earth and my presence

I've been obliquely
sliding into cartography

a standstill moon   three times
in a lifespan   once more in mine

the same lines in my own
home place by the sea

monographs ask
how could they do it

but memory is a bird
that flies from tree to tree

what it knows other birds know
and it isn't fragile

POST SCRIPT

February, St. Peter's Abbey, Muenster, Saskatchewan

Minus 25 and snowing—brings eighteen deer
into the stubble between here and the cemetery
for better grazing. I send emails
to a friend up the road, and the words

...the path I am on sound strange
but also correct. How should I do this?
Write from the heart, one artist tells me.
Give me a song, says the *Pietà* in clay of another.

Just last week, a friend I thought an atheist
spoke of sacred moments.
Sacred, she said. Shift a word
and the world shifts with it.

And I, I need the lost not to be lost.
I want the small voices back
that talked to me, a drifting
leaf, those friendly crows.

A country away from where it started
I need the snow, the wind that keeps me
in my room thinking. I need the cursor blinking
on a page that doesn't yet exist, but will.

PART 2

Little Voices

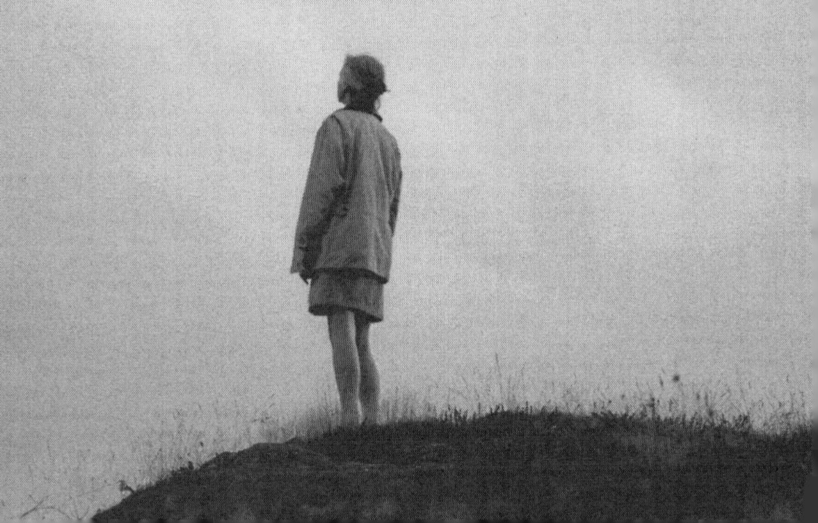

LITTLE VOICES

A voice carries all that we are. It wears no mask. But what do I make of the long list of people I have known—enough to fill a village—who had no voices, those who lost part or all of their speech? What I remember most is not their silence, but their presence. I think of them often.

ANNE

My sister Anne is twenty months older than me. She has a grown daughter and a grandchild now. Spinal meningitis destroyed her hearing when she was three. My father was a teacher in Castlegar, in the interior of southern British Columbia. He liked to fish from the boulder-strewn shore of the Columbia River. Our neighbour kept cutthroat trout in a bathtub out in his yard. I helped to wash the juicy strawberries my mother sliced into the steaming canning kettle that turned them into swirls of sweet, dark jam. My brothers and sisters played on the lawn while my father shut himself into the veranda, where he typed out the next great Canadian play. The spools of the black Royal Underwood typewriter made a pleasing whirring sound as he rewound the ribbon dented by the steel faces of the letters in the new masterpiece. The bell rang and the carriage made a satisfying *chunk* each time it returned to start a new line.

The meningitis struck somewhere in the middle of this sunny idyll. The bacterial form is the most serious strain. It attacks the membrane surrounding the brain and can cause kidney damage, blindness, seizures, developmental delay, septicemia leading to amputations, and sometimes death. It left my sister with complete hearing loss. Children who are not born deaf may come to believe that their parents' voices are broken, or that their mothers and fathers have deliberately stopped talking to them. Anne probably saw it that way. She couldn't walk at first and had to drag herself across the floor. It took her months to learn to walk again. She tells me now that music is the thing she missed most, and still misses. I remember none of this. I simply withdrew from this strange new person, whose shape appeared seizing whatever toy it wanted with no explanation.

The twenty-something social worker told us that Anne would have to go to a school for the deaf in Vancouver. My father painted a cedar trunk with red enamel paint so that Anne would be able to see it in the airport if she got lost. I played quietly as my mother stitched labels onto my sister's socks and blouses and folded them into the trunk. Anne was excited the first time we took her to the airport. It was hardly more than a shed next to a runway guarded by a chain-link fence. My father packed the whole family into the car to see her and my mother off. We watched the trunk being loaded into the gleaming belly of the DC-3. My mother came back a week later. I was hazy about where Anne had gone. It was as if we all had been holding our breath for a long, long time and were finally allowed to exhale.

I was in my teens when my mother started to tell the whole story—what happens to a deaf child who is taken to a school in a far-off city and left there. At first, my mother flew to Vancouver to visit her on weekends. My sister thought she'd be going home only to be left behind. Anne soon learned what the red trunk meant. When my sister was home and it was time to go back to school, my mother had to pack it in secret when Anne was in bed. I shouldn't have been up, but I remember watching this. The point was to delay the tantrums as the time to leave got closer. Anne started getting up in the middle of the night to make sure my mother wasn't packing the trunk while she was sleeping.

> This is a ball glove. Can you
> say that, Anne?
> ball. glove. *Aawl uhf.*
> Again.
> *Aawl uhf.*
> Again.
> *Aawl uhf.*

Very young children do something called parallel play. They will play beside each other in the same room but are unable to play cooperatively or imagine the other child's world; they are separate beings in the same room. Our lives have been like that. Anne came and went for the next twenty years, first to schools for the deaf, then to Gallaudet University in Washington, DC. She lives in Nova Scotia now. Because of language and years spent apart, I have never had a deep conversation with Anne or even a long ordinary one. Still, I picked up signs without knowing it. I don't realize it until I see a deaf couple in conversation in a restaurant. I study their hands and faces; it's like a language I know deep down but have somehow forgotten.

TREKKER

We left BC and moved to Prince Albert, Saskatchewan. A few years later, my father got a job as director of a training school for adults with intellectual disabilities. It was a converted TB hospital, and I was one of the hospital rats—staff kids in the background of black and white snapshots of training school picnics and ball games. Between my father's work and mine, I have seen the inside of at least twenty institutions for children, psychiatric hospitals, veterans' hospitals, rehabilitation centres, care homes, and closed units for those in the last stages of dementia. Some of these places were modern with leading-edge therapies and a liberal view of patients' rights. Others were gloomy bastions, a dreary maze of hallways, side rooms, and steam pipes leading to back wards that belonged in the nineteenth century. Most fell somewhere in the vast middle.

> A city of ghosts at the end
> of the municipal road. Telling this now
> I say to myself, I owe them, owe them something.

My father started his job with a tour of all the institutions in the province in 1961. Weyburn Mental Hospital in southeast Saskatchewan was supposed to be the highlight. The use of new psychotropic drugs and behaviour-shaping techniques were finally providing effective treatments and reversing the effects of decades of institutionalization. Densely typeset monographs described how catatonic patients who never left their beds, even for meals, were coaxed in carefully analyzed steps, first to get up, then to walk to the cafeteria. Gradually, they regained something resembling the outline of themselves that the hospital, not the illness, had knocked out of them.

My father picked out an older man he wanted to speak to. The guide assured him that the fellow was mute. All the same, my father went over and began speaking to him. The cadre of VIPs was stunned when the man began to answer the questions—his name, where he came from, and how long he had been there. The man had been there since the Regina Riot of July 1, 1935. The riot was provoked when three hundred RCMP attacked a rally of On-to-Ottawa trekkers and 1,500 local supporters protesting the slave-like conditions in relief camps for the unemployed. The trekkers were riding the rails to take their protest to Ottawa. Prime Minister R.B. Bennett ordered the RCMP to stop them in Regina. At least two people were killed.

> Just wherever they could, they hit him
> they were hitting him on the head and wherever
> they could—arms and everything. He was
> smothered in blood. You couldn't see
> who he was, you could see he was
> a man, and I saw one that I
> know, Sergeant Terry Logan, and I said, *What*
> *are you trying to do, are you*
> *trying to kill him*?
>
> —Testimony, Regina Riot Witness[1]

The jails soon filled. Someone decided to send the remaining trekkers to the province's mental hospitals. The man my father picked out was still there twenty-six years later. There is no way to know why the fellow started to speak after all this time. Perhaps it was because my father didn't look like a doctor. The jargon of the day would call this the effect of a new stimulus. Or perhaps it was random and after spending half of his life in the place, the man simply decided his silence should end. The exile come home at last.

THUNDERBIRD

Children who live in staff houses on the edge of institutions quickly get used to the shy human shapes wandering the sports fields and rolling lawns fronting these places. We imitated our parents, joking and cajoling the residents for some kind of response. We were "flies on the wall" who heard staff talking about their cases, whether one person knew what month it was, or another who was a good worker that could be left alone. It wasn't the story of Nurse Ratched from *One Flew Over the Cuckoo's Nest,* but for now, these places were still in operation. The Prince Albert Training School had a summer camp with a curving quartz-white beach in the provincial forest an hour northeast of town. Camp Thunderbird had a bunkhouse, boat launch, and combined dining hall and dorm. The rule was that every resident should have a week's vacation at the camp. Fishing parties went out in two motorboats. My father named one the *Lazy Loon,* after a boat he had as a kid. The other was christened the *I'm Alone,* after a Canadian rum-runner sunk in international waters by the US Coastguard in 1929.

Camp life was captured on a 16-millimetre film that I still watch once in a while. I see the muscular Cree man we used to call Big Joe. There must have been other First Nation residents, but he is the one I remember. He was rough-shaven and towered over us kids with a questioning smile. Joe carried the lumber and held sheets of plywood in place when the camp was built. He always wanted to please and was looking for something to do, so one of the staff said in an off-handed way, "Why don't you dig a hole for the outhouse?"

Joe disappeared and hours later he was found up to his neck in a hole twenty feet in front of the main hall. Staff told him to fill it in, then staked out where it should go. Joe didn't seem to mind. By the end of the second day, he dug a pit big enough for a luxurious three-holer and had to come out when water started to seep in around his boots. Watching the film, I can see he was the kind of person who easily could have lived in a community home. The outhouse story was a joke around the camp for a long time. Sometimes people become caricatures defined by some action or gesture. It's human nature to create narratives of the mysterious other as the actual person disappears. I often wonder what happened to Joe when he got old and could no longer walk effortlessly along a springing plank with a wheelbarrow full of cement. What happened to that thick black hair, to the weathered brown face and impenetrable grin? Joe would never guess he is part of this story.

He comes from a lost race
of giants, forest dwellers
who walked out of the forest—
so the boy believes.

"Dig a hole here," Staff says.
Joe digs and keeps on digging. Staff
tells him to stop. "How are you going to
get out of that hole, Joe?"

Joe looks up grinning, the form
of an uneasy thought in his mind as he shifts
from foot to foot, his black
running shoes soaked by groundwater as it
gushes into each huge print.

What does the boy make of it?
That in a day Joe can dig a hole deeper
than a man. "Planning to sleep
in there, Joe?" Staff says.
"Staying for lunch?"
If reason is all that counts, the boy
is older than Joe, feels a child's
instinct to protect.

A muscle
does what is asked.
Joe is already part
of a child's history of remembering.

Years from now the boy
will dig his own garden, look
where the blade of the shovel
frowns as it stands in the dirt. He already senses
the way lives graze one another.

We look back through dark matter
to find where we are. Anomalies
in the wave fields of Heaven.

Thunderbird campers were expected to rest during Quiet Hour. Many spent half their lives in the predictable routine of the institution and needed the calm after supper. They were stressed by the constant demands and the all-day socializing. It was difficult to know what to do with one large woman. Her name was Emily. Staff worried they might not be able to manage her in the rustic facilities, but they tried anyway. She could respond to her name but even that wasn't certain. She never spoke during the two summers I knew her. During Quiet Hour, they led her to an Adirondack chair set between pines on a low crest of sand overlooking the lake. Emily sat there alone. I was only twelve but one of the nurses made it my job to watch her while the other campers were lying down in the dorm. At some point she would begin to yodel and carry on until rest time was over and it was time to stop. It wasn't the comic yodel one hears from hayseed characters on corny TV shows. It was a sweet, virtuosic song that rose and fell, and was made for the distances of the lake. It flew out over the brimming water, waiting for the answer that came when the stillness was right.

Anne was hired as a camp counsellor for two summers. My father must have had a hand in it. It's the only time I have known him to use his work to help any of his kids. That was his code. He may have been an atheist, but there was more of the minister's son in him than he would ever admit. The job worked out fine. Anne already knew the campers and seemed to have no problem communicating with them even though her speech isn't as clear as it is for some deaf people. She ran the motorboat by setting the choke and giving the starter cord one good pull. She adjusted the throttle by laying the flat of her hand on the top of the motor so she could feel the vibrations. My sister was a powerful swimmer. One of the staff was an avid scuba diver and gave Anne lessons. She told us she was frightened by a huge pike lurking almost motionless in the jack weeds where the sandy shallows offshore finally dropped down. Even before Thunderbird, she dove and swam for hours beyond the dock of my grandparents' cabin. It's just a fragment of memory—or maybe a wish—but I see her swimming the lake, with me close by in the rowboat watching, though I'm not the one at the oars.

a skyful of light   water deep
you swim

a slightly bent   grace
your arm

reaches out
fingers

apart
reaching in

you shoulder
a weight   that hasn't arrived

the boat is not moving

FIONA

I met Fiona when I lived Down East. I was a mental health volunteer in Dartmouth, Nova Scotia. I worked at a Boys and Girls Club. Fiona was so sedentary that I guessed she was at least thirty years old. I found out later she was only twenty, and younger than me. She liked to sit at the end of the couch in the main room of the White Cross Centre, which was really just a converted house with a Canadian Mental Health sign on the lawn. She wore an Alice blue dress with small white daisies swirling about the fabric. Her plump, round face lit up when her favourite volunteer came into the room. Fiona could have been anyone's *baba*. I was told she was functioning at the level of a four-year-old, but the mistakes I have seen make me skeptical of these kinds of pronouncements.

Fiona was born in rural Nova Scotia. Two decades into deinstitionalization, stories of Dickensian county homes where unwed mothers and people like Fiona were sent were still fresh in everyone's mind. The most infamous case was the Ideal Maternity Home in East Chester.[2] The home was owned by William and Lila Young. It was supposed to provide care for pregnant single mothers and to help adopt out the babies. All through the 1930s and '40s the babies were actually being sold to couples in the US for as much as ten thousand dollars. The children of both unwed mothers and married couples were sold in this way. Sometimes the parents were told the child had died after delivery. Babies who couldn't be sold were allowed to starve to death on a diet of molasses and water. The emaciated bodies were buried in butter boxes on the grounds of the Home, burned in the furnace, or simply tossed into the ocean.

Fiona's parents kept her shut up in the house. People must have known she was there. Maybe something happened when it was time for her to go to school. But Fiona spent the next fifteen years in the children's wing of the Nova Scotia Hospital in Dartmouth. She was finally placed in a boarding home. She had no speech when she was referred to the White Cross Centre. Members and volunteers came and went through the week. One of the staff played the upright piano in the living room and there was a sing-along almost every night. He started to teach Fiona to play a few simple tunes. The music made its way in. She began to hum, then slowly, she started to speak. We asked her questions that she answered with a short, "Yes," or "No," or a three-word sentence. The object was to draw language out of her. Few experiences compare with unearthing a voice in this way. You want to hear it again as if it might disappear at any moment and be gone for good. And maybe it could be. Fiona was lucky. For people who never got out, a story like this one is the only proof they ever existed.

JERRY

I met Jerry Rush when I moved back to Saskatchewan after ten years in the Maritimes. Jerry was born in ranch country in Saskatchewan's arid southwest. We were both new poets in a writing group we named the Correction Line after the jog surveyors make in a road going north to adjust for the convergence of lines of longitude as they approach the pole. Jerry's first teaching job was in what is now Nunavut. The Canadian government had just ordered the traditional Inuit to bring their children in off the land to go to school in settlements across the North. The families moved with them. Jerry's school was in Igloolik, a ten-mile-long island in Fury and Hecla Strait between the Melville Peninsula and Baffin Island. It's in the middle of a traditional hunting ground a hundred kilometres inside the Arctic Circle. Igloolik means "there is a house here." Inuit people have been there almost continuously for four thousand years.

Three years after we started our writing group, Jerry developed a cough he couldn't get rid of. The doctor thought it was a throat infection. There wasn't much pain, but the cough carried on for months. Finally, it was diagnosed as cancer of the larynx. Jerry's treatment took him to the Mayo Clinic, but in the end, he had to go to Princess Margaret Hospital in Toronto for a laryngectomy. No one said it, but it was hard to think of him never being able to read his own work. We never spoke of what else might be coming. It should have been natural for me to reach out to him—I'm the one with the deaf sister after all—but it wasn't. I can't say what the others were thinking, I only know that I waited longer than I should have to call Jerry's wife, June, and make arrangements to go over. Even now, I can see the three of us in my mind, from a point somewhere above the kitchen table. I remind myself to be looking at Jerry when I'm speaking and try not to count on June to fill in the silences while he's writing. It feels familiar—this space between what's almost there and what's missing. Like a restart of my life with Anne. Once more I'm that kid reduced to a gesture, passing notes at the table, my vocabulary swollen—and it isn't from cortisone.

Jerry was working on his new book, *The Bones of Their Occasion.*[3] He invited me to travel with him to Igloolik, where he planned to do some writing based on his time there. We left in late September and flew from Montréal up the east side of Hudson Bay. The treeline disappeared. The plane set down in Iqaluit to take on more passengers. We flew from there to the gravel runway at Hall Beach (now Sanirajak). A row of blue prefab trailers was raised off the ground at the side of the runway. It must have been to get above the twelve-foot reach of a polar bear. We switched to a Twin Otter and crossed Fury and Hecla Strait on the short flight to Igloolik. The landing was rough. When we walked down the steps, we saw a small plane with its nose stabbed into the ground past the end of the runway. The airport crew couldn't remove the wreck until the crash investigation team arrived, so they pushed it to the edge of the landing strip. The pilot never walked away.

Igloolik is a low, treeless island. Flat pieces of limestone rise and fall under a thin blanket of lichen, moss, and cotton grass. Walking in summer is hard on the joints and treacherous. Travel over the ice in winter is much easier. One overcast afternoon, I walked with Jerry toward the northern tip of the island. We discovered the remains of a caribou near a gentle crease in the land. All that remained were two rows of stained, upward-pointing ribs held together by strips of sinew and membrane. Three tumbled inuksuit in the distance were part of the story.

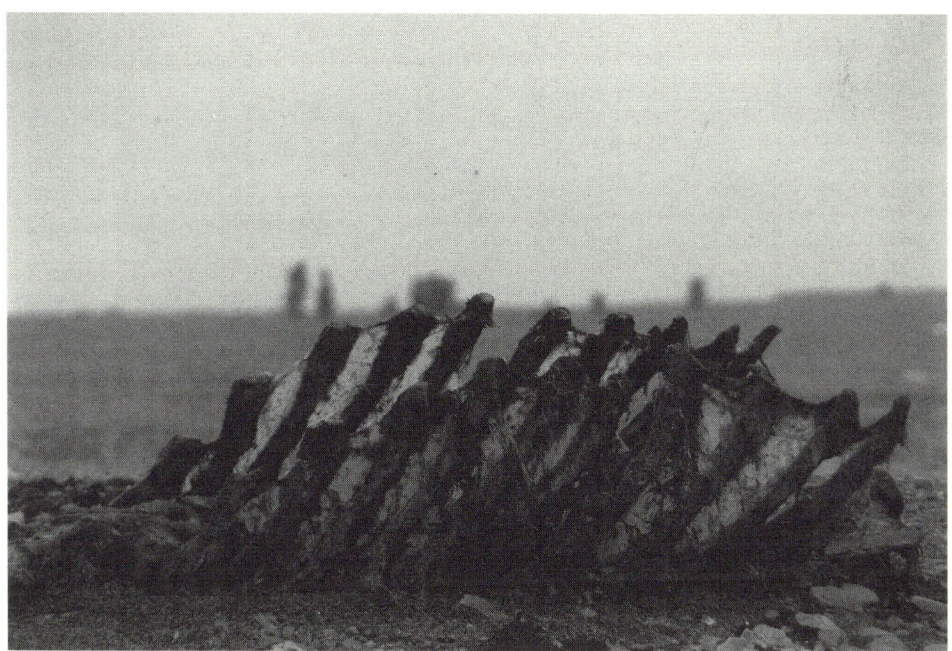

Caribou carcass. Igloolik, Nunavut.
Photo by Bruce Rice.

We could see how the undulation of the land must have guided the animal to its doom. I was surprised to find the scene so close to town. Unlike the postcard images one sees in the south, the three stone figures had no arms. They were stacked up with what could be found and pried loose. I still have the picture of Jerry standing beside them with his walking stick, the fourth inuksuk. When we got home, we asked a young Inuk fellow we knew why all this was so close to town. He never really answered. He was more interested in telling his own story, which confirmed what others said about him.

Charlie Uttuk
climbs the hill
research station
out of sight, no
inuksuk here
so he
builds one. It makes
the anthropologists
nuts he says. People just
laugh, "Well, that's Charlie."

We were billeted in a one-room cabin with an oil stove that heated the place up quickly. The Oblate mission built it for the Grey Nuns, who visited the settlement from time to time. Two girls and a boy with his front baby teeth missing came to the door. They stood in the middle of the kitchen and lined up behind Jerry as I took their picture. They were fascinated by the portable Brothers typewriter. They watched as Jerry typed, the bell ringing and the letters flying onto the page. I kept a journal but never wrote anything of consequence. We wandered the edges of town. Jerry ate Pilot biscuits and drank sludgy nutrient mix from a can. Our host, Father Robert Lechat, kept to himself in the main building except for the night we tried to watch the Blue Jays on a snowy television set. Meanwhile, the real snow—the clinking of ice out on Turton Bay (Ikpiarjuk) and the freeze-up everyone was waiting for—was starting outside.

I decided to attend Sunday mass as a courtesy to our host, but I also wanted to meet people in a more natural situation. Jerry said he didn't want to go. I wasn't sure if he wasn't feeling well or if he just wanted some time to himself. The limestone church next to our cabin was nothing like the low, flat matchbox buildings everyone lived in. The half-arch of the stonework face caught the hard Arctic light. An ivory Christ carved from a walrus tusk watched from its cross over the door. Father Lechat said the building took three days to heat up and wasn't used any more, except at Easter. It turned out that the real church was a simple, well-insulated building with four rows of white panels screwed into the ceiling, blue walls, and clear-paned windows shipped in from the south. The wide cedar pews were custom-built to accommodate families in northern wear. I sat two-thirds of the way to the back, where people made a space for me next to the aisle. The hymns were sung in Inuktitut, which rolls as it rises and falls, and seems to have been made for singing. We sat with our parkas open, warmed by the diffused morning light. Perfectly stitched wall hangings hung above the altar. The felt animals were behaving as they did in life: a ringed seal lazing on an ice floe, a caribou, a polar bear and arctic fox, a musk ox, a walrus, and bowhead whale. Each scene was framed with matching words of the Psalms, beginning with *The birds of the air praise Him,* in gold cloth syllabics. The harder the land the softer the language.

Our translator was the granddaughter of Noah Piugattuk, an old hunter and one of the two oldest men in the village. He fell through the thin edge ice while hunting seals when he was younger, but somehow survived. I took notes as we interviewed him. I worked a small recorder and added questions to the ones Jerry wrote down. People were glad to see him. He brought back memories of the old days when they had just come in from the land. We were asking about things they liked to remember, as their daughters and grandchildren poured tea and listened across the table.

Jerry finished his manuscript when we got home. He wrote some good poems, but I always wondered if he expected more from the effort. The cancer progressed and he died a month before the book was published. His voice blurs when I try to remember it, but I see his face clearly. Even his body seemed to be listening as he leaned toward me. He was finding a way. One of his last poems says:

> Little voice, speak like a friend
> smiling under her heavy load.
> Sing sweet and low like
> snow quilting Christmas Eve.
> ...

Now that I have begun to know you, know me,
it is as if I have found a healer I can trust.
Tomorrow will be worthwhile without us. Little voice
stay as long as you can, stay with me.

—Jerry Rush, "After Reading 'Madrigal' by Felix Grande"

LEARNING TO SIGN

Our voice is always with us. This is what my father must have known when he approached that On-to-Ottawa trekker in the Weyburn hospital, although he didn't expect the result. I look for a meaning in the accumulation of all these lives. I don't want to believe that it's random, but maybe it is. I work with words, but I am constantly reminded there is more than one kind of language. I visited Anne's school only once. I remember deaf boys playing catch in the fenced-in courtyard. The enclosed space seemed to concentrate the joy they unleashed with a physicality that made me envious. It wasn't each other's voices they heard as the small yellow football spiraled in high arcs across the yard, it was the percussions in their own bodies. I felt it too as I watched from the side. I still feel the connection with families I never met when I drive past the yellow diamond of a sign on a residential street with a simple caution, *Deaf Child*. I slow down to look for a ball rolling onto the street, for the child as I pass.

Rationally, I understand that my sister's deafness is a disability, but the truth is that I have known Anne this way all my life and even now I think of it as normal. I've known so many on the other side of speech: that trekker in Weyburn, whose story my father told so many times it's as if I knew him myself; Big Joe; Emily playing that donated piano in the White Cross Centre; Fiona by the lake; that photo I keep of Jerry pointing at our cabin's useless address, number 157, beside a peeling blue door sixty miles inside the Arctic Circle; and more. Telling it now, I see this is my story too. Beyond words, language requires our presence. It implies a sense of the other. I remember the voices and their effort to shape a few words into a simple sentence. My heart still races when I think of the frustration, the mass of my own baffled silence, and the sense of failure when I just couldn't "get it"—the thin line between the loss of speech and the loss of a voice. The signs are addressed to me.

PART 3

Song of the Lark

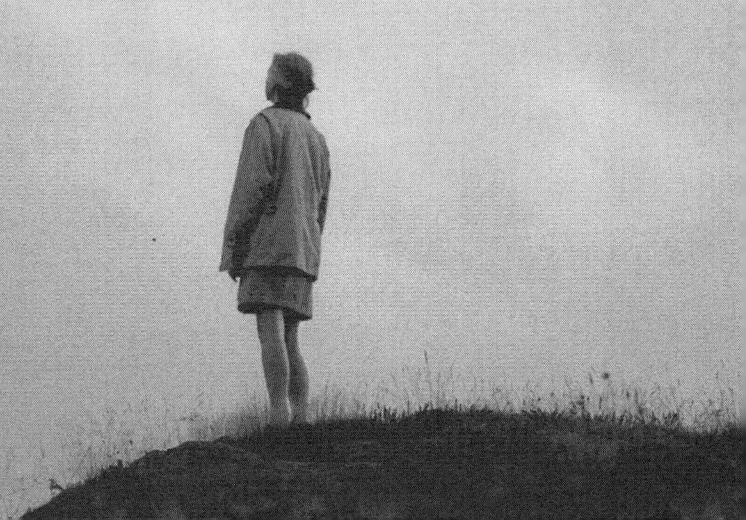

CHICAGO

His clothes are clean enough. And the jacket is new but there's something frayed-looking about the young man. It could be the reckless surge of hair, but it's more than that. He walks without haste but with a clear sense of direction. This is downtown Chicago and he's heading toward the lake. His act in the comedy club has just bombed. The only thing he just killed is his career. For some reason he can't explain just now, he changes course and turns up Michigan Avenue, toward the familiar steps of the Art Institute. He stops with no memory of how he got here, in front of a painting, *Song of the Lark.* Inside the gilt frame, a young peasant woman stands alone in a field. She pauses in the still-tentative dawn and looks to the side, listening to something in the part of the field we can't see. The early light brings the tiled roof of a half-hidden farmhouse forward from the thick line of trees in the distance. The woman's arms rest at her side. She holds the sickle loosely. The song of the lark vibrates like a reed in the first breathing of the field, in the ordinary beauty a life like hers requires. She has not yet been bent by the work to come.

In an interview decades later, a BBC host will ask actor and comedian Bill Murray if a work of art has ever changed his life. Murray continues the story with full candor.

> *I just walked inside [the Institute] and I didn't feel I had any place being there...and I just walked right through it because I was ready to die—and pretty much dead. And I walked in and there's a painting there...it's a woman working in a field and there's a sunrise behind her. I've always loved this painting. I saw it that day and I just thought, well look, there's a girl without a whole lot of prospects but the sun's coming up anyway and she's got another chance at it. I think that gave me some sort of feeling that I too am a person and I get another chance every day the sun comes up.*

Jules Breton could never have guessed that his quiet painting, the tones and time of day he loved so well, would reach across the ocean to save the life he would never meet a century later. Breton was simply doing what he did every day, one of many works beginning with a sketch en plein air then finished in the studio. Murray's story catches his interviewer off guard.

Perhaps it's the actor's way of sending a message to himself and who he was then, the residue of healing that's never quite finished. There's no way to predict when a work of art might step into a life like this, but we recognize the effect—how a certain song heard over and over, or a painting or poem, settles into our lives like a sea anchor without our knowing it's there. Sinking deep, it holds us to our bearings in hard times and sometimes it saves us.

NATALIE MACMASTER

Natalie MacMaster, Cape Breton's much-loved gift to Celtic Music and one of the best fiddlers to ever come from that island, stands on the open-air stage of the Regina Folk Festival. The setting sun illuminates the top of City Hall behind her. The long rays catch on the crowns of the elms lining the walks of Victoria Park and sink into the tinted windows of the twin towers on 12th Ave. Halfway through her set, MacMaster stops to tell the story of the tune she's about to play. It's for an old man and his wife that she met while the couple was revisiting the place they loved in the early days of their marriage. For years, they promised to go back to but never had. His wife had dementia now. The husband was determined to keep the promise that had fallen to him. Natalie goes further. She tells us about the letters she's received from hundreds of people writing to say they've been moved by her music and how it helped them through a difficult time. These are the tunes of a beloved place, perhaps even a blood memory that takes people who will always be *from back home* back to a farm, a bit of shore, or the legendary bridge in a family tale even if they, themselves, have *never been*. She tells the thousand or so people in lawn chairs, those lying on blankets and standing in the walkway, that all this has little to do with her. It's about how music works and has little to do, she says, with whatever skill she might have. She says the word *skill* as if it's a diminutive. It's a glimpse of the life behind the veil of performance. She speaks with an openheartedness about something that is so completely a part of her; music's reach into our lives, its way of finding the place that needs it most. Then she lifts her fiddle in the last of the magic hour, as the warm August evening finds its way home.

CALISTOGA, CALIFORNIA

In my early days as a poet imbued with the naïf ambition of most new writers, I signed up for the Napa Valley Writers Conference in St. Helena, California. The conference was actually a workshop led by some rising and quite famous American writers—Ron Carlson, Mark Doty, Brenda Hillman, Nick Flynn, and others.[1] I was looking for a taste of American writing culture and how different it must be from the one I knew. It was the deep end of the pool and part of me wanted to know if my own work would make any kind of impression at all. The faculty readings were held at the Napa Valley wineries, including a grand Spanish-style winery that could easily have held five hundred people under the high arches of its hacienda-style reception room. American writers are great readers of their own work. Unlike the poor cousins of "British literature" here in the colonies, there is nothing deferential in the way they present themselves. They are expected to speak for the culture, a shift that has finally started to take hold in Canada.

The highlight of my US adventure came from Chick Harrity and Yvonne Henry, the couple I was billeted with. They lived on the outskirts of Calistoga, a town just eight miles from the conference. Chick and Yvonne were both photographers. Chick was a retired Associated Press photographer and had a small studio that was hardly more than a shed set in the half-shade of the ponderosa pines behind the house. One afternoon, he invited me into his studio and brought out a three-ring binder filled with his AP photographs slipped into archival sleeves. He began flipping through the remarkable set of photos from the days when he had close access to US presidents in a way that would be unthinkable now. As a White House photojournalist, he covered every president from John F. Kennedy to Bill Clinton.

There was a photo of JFK with his family on a balcony a couple of weeks before his assassination. Chick paused at a close-up of Martin Luther King speaking into a row of microphones before the March on Washington, and an eye-level photograph of Gerald Ford swimming directly into the camera as he does laps in the White House pool. Then came the iconic image of Richard Milhous Nixon with his face contorted in a way that can't be unseen. This may be the photograph that a former White House staffer said they hid from the president for almost a week until Nixon finally demanded to see it, and promptly exploded. Then we came to the photograph that stirred the country.

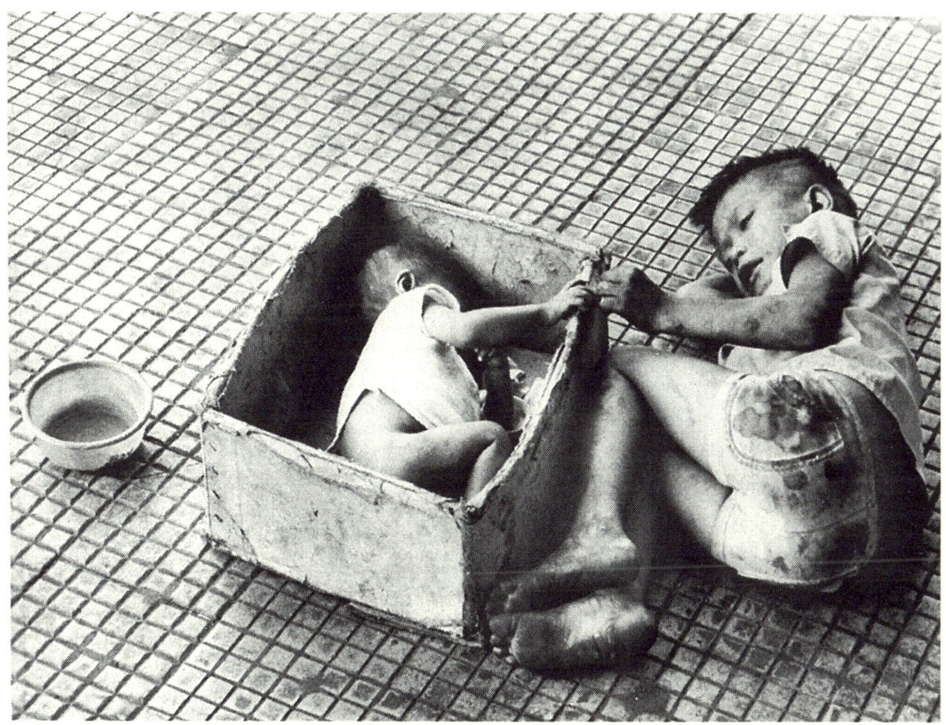

Baby in a Box. Tran Thie Het Nhanny (now Nhanny Heil), her brother beside her.
Photo by Chick Harrity, Saigon 1973. Associated Press. Reproduced with permission.

Chick was in Saigon in 1973 covering the Vietnam War. He was on his way to a briefing with some generals when he spotted a young boy curled up on the sidewalk next to a box that held his baby sister. Chick said the driver was probably with the Viet Cong, who had infiltrated everywhere, and was as anxious to get to the briefing as he was. Harrity made him pull over anyway and took the shot. The photo went out over the wire. It became one of the most memorable images from Vietnam. When "Baby in a Box" appeared in the US press, people wanted to know who she was and what happened to her. The search began and Chick guessed it may have been the Viet Cong who actually found her, which is how things worked at the time. It turned out she had a heart murmur. When people found out, they sent in money to fly her to the States where she had the operation that saved her life. An American family adopted her. Years later, Nhanny, the child in the photograph, presented Harrity with the lifetime achievement award for the White House News Photographers Association.

The world has been moved by photographs before, and this one sticks. As Chick finishes turning the pages he says to me, "Well, I guess this is my so-called career." His voice stayed low. We let the conversation pause for a bit. What I remember most is how he still seemed to be working through the memory of that box that could barely hold the child sleeping inside it, and what it still weighed. Surely a story like this leaves a mark on the one doing the saving. Not a scar exactly, but a measure of who a person is in that moment, the kind of thing one still speaks about quietly thirty years later. As if it happened to someone else.

TASH SULTANA RECORDING AT HOME

Tash Sultana works barefoot in her studio, taking a few quick steps to set up the looping array. She plays guitar with a finger-tapping style. She keeps it simple. Adds some keys and percussion. Tash was able to quit busking on Melbourne's famous Bourke Street after the bedroom recording of her song "Jungle" went viral with over 150 million views. She was just nineteen at the time. Music like this touches thousands, but sometimes it's the artist who needs saving. Tash made it past drug-induced psychosis at seventeen and says quite frankly, "I would be in the gutter somewhere if I didn't have music. I would be dead." She keeps working, doesn't even look at the camera as she says this, loops a simple chord progression from her guitar, then comes back and plays a line over it. She's almost ready for the vocals. It's a penetrating effect. One can easily understand the hundreds of fan posts, many with the real names of people her music helped through tough times. One says, "This song got me through my darkest days of addiction. I played this song over & over while I was detoxing. 5 years clean." This is all it takes to let others, and maybe themselves, know they're okay now. The posts scroll by in a narrative of recovery.

I think of my own grown kids as I watch her work. They're just a bit older than she is. I remember their friend who slept on the couch in our basement for a few weeks, and how funny his size 13 shoes looked beside ours. His parents tossed him out, so he wound up with us. We hardly knew he was there. He only showed up to sleep and moved out before long. He seemed to be making his way. Three years later—no one knows what happened—he drowned in the prairie lake an hour from town. It was unbelievably simple. He was joking as he dove in and it all seemed fine. He simply disappeared without coming up. There was never an explanation; his friends think he hit a log and knocked himself out. They said more at his funeral than his mother or father, who said almost nothing. But what right way is there for these things to be done anyway? It was a weird sermon—all about final judgment. If there was any wisdom or consolation to be found, it came from those young people, and not from the pastor. There are posts like this on Tash's video. I don't know who wrote them, but it feels like I might.

These days, the compassionate, private stories of youth and their difficult generation are drowned out as if they are lesser than the ones that grab headlines. What room can possibly be left for some high school kid trying to deal with a first death close to them. Others a bit older have come through suicide, and here they are online trying to lift their story into something better, and themselves along with it. Tapping notes into phones, some are simply trying to swim through the day. The Tash Sultanas of this world, in their studios and in their music, are making a person-size, daylit space—a commons where all these breaths held in can be let go. Where things can be spoken of. And where the Songs of Experience feel like their experience.

PABLO NERUDA

The world knows Ricardo Eliécer Neftalí Reyes Basoalto as Pablo Neruda. The Chilean poet born in 1904 received the Nobel Prize for Literature in 1971, but even that didn't save him from being poisoned two years later by Chile's dictator, General Augusto Pinochet. Neruda was the Chilean Consul in Madrid when the Spanish Civil War broke out in 1936. Germany and Italy immediately came in on the side of the Nationalists and General Franco who fought to overthrow the democratically elected Republican government. The art world remembers the war through Pablo Picasso's monumental *Guernica,* painted in 1937. His stark 3.5 by 7.8 metre work in oil memorializes the Basque town of five thousand people that was bombed by the German Condor Legion on Franco's orders. One estimate says that a third of the population was killed. That same year, Neruda published his most political book, *Spain in Our Hearts* (*España en el Corazón*). The poems were written as he witnessed the atrocities of the war, and following the murder of his friend and poet, Federico García Lorca.

The actual book is remarkable. It had to be printed in secret. As the war dragged on, the Republicans had to make everything. When they ran out of paper for printing the book, they made their own, including some that was made from the bloodstained shirt of a Zouave soldier on the Nationalist side. They kept the book with them as they escaped across the border into France, where many were seized. Franco's soldiers destroyed the area where the press was located. The fate of the Zouave soldier's shirt is the very definition of a talisman: using some possession of the slain enemy to hold back evil and to absolve the bearer. This dangerous book is what people on the run took with them—essential as food and what little else they could carry.

The story seems extraordinary. But isn't it possible to imagine ourselves doing the same in a time that may yet come, when our only passport is our courage?

A MIDNIGHT DREAM: BACK IN KISISKÂCIWAN/SASKATCHEWAN

ahāw,
ōta ka-wīhtamātin ācimisowin
I will share these stories
but I will not share
those from which I will never crawl.
It is best that way.

—Louise Bernice Halfe – Sky Dancer,
"Dedication to the Seventh Generation"

Louise Bernice Halfe – Sky Dancer (Cree), Canada's ninth national poet laureate, begins her book *Burning in This Midnight Dream*[2] with this introduction to her healing journey as a residential school survivor. Louise was born in Two Hills, Alberta, and grew up on Saddle Lake Reserve. She was forced to attend Blue Quills Residential School at age seven. The poems ask nothing for herself. Weep for those who were lost she says, and for "those who haven't yet sung."

Louise lives in Saskatchewan now. I met her years ago when we signed up for a writing program held in a Franciscan retreat overlooking a side branch of the Qu'Appelle Valley. Weather systems and high-flying migrations of snow geese and arctic swans follow the valley as it cuts across the province. The Qu'Appelle drops down suddenly from grain fields up top, its coulees forested by tough burr oak and scrub. I remember Louise keeping slightly apart with those poems inside her, her door in the dim hallway closed. Something was happening in there and whatever it was wasn't easy.

Louise was an established poet by the time *Midnight Dream* was published in 2016, just months after the release of the TRC report[3] on Canada's Indian residential schools. She writes, *I don't like walking backwards*; but she does it so her fellow survivors understand the fault isn't theirs. She says, *I am often filled by ghosts / that flow through my body.*[4] These dreams and visions are more than metaphors. The poet has given so much, and what's on the page is only part of it.

Mezzanine of Regina Public Library (RPL)

Her reading done, Louise Bernice Halfe – Sky Dancer makes her way among the well-wishers and old friends. The audience breaks into clusters that block the narrow route along a half-wall to the escalator. It forces anyone who wants to leave to squeeze by. We're used to the space and no one complains. I recognize other writers, First Nation and Métis community people I know from my old day job at the City, and the usual library and event staff. But most of the faces are new. I let the crowd thin before I make my way over to say hello.

Another writer, Carla Harris, approaches from the opposite direction. She seems to have made up her mind about something. The three of us know each other. I nod to Carla and mouth a simple *Hi* without saying it. She thanks Louise for the reading, and then says, "I just wanted to tell you that *Burning in This Midnight Dream* saved me." Carla will tell me later that she never planned any of this. She simply wasn't prepared for the effect the reading would have. Carla was the victim of a sexual assault that dragged through the justice system for two and a half years. I backed off so she could tell Louise what she needed to. With her permission, I can share what she recently said about *Midnight Dream* and that afternoon in the library.[5]

> *She helped me see that I was sliding into depression. There isn't one day, no clear single sound that rings from you to warn you about your mental wellness. The change comes slowly…It has taken me so many years of writing about that period to fully be able to understand what I went through. It drifts in so gradually that it's easy not to notice and the way you look outward from your body has changed. I was going for massages, I had to wrap my wrists because I was having such violent nerve pinches. I was having more & more migraines, and more and more seizures. I had not yet made any connection between all these bad days, and maybe that this sadness & anger & tension were coming from somewhere, from a dark line of thought that needed to be released and helped to heal.*
>
> *That was when I picked up* Burning in This Midnight Dream *one day when I was walking through the RPL. I flipped the book open to decide if I should borrow it & opened to the first poem, "Dedication to the Seventh Generation." The first stanza gripped me on something, the difference between stories from my life that I would share, and these*

dark ones that I was caught in, that I was pushing away. I kept reading. I felt my mind turn in the next poem when she spoke of the "tough mistress of confusion."

When I was depressed…I thought no one would see me or look at me, or ask anything from me, and this would be the only way to not be attacked again & again. After many times of reading some of her poems I realized that it was just the internal pain she was describing, the fear and the flashing between memory & now: that trauma can be from very different sources, but there are many things about the experience of being in the pain which can be emotionally shared. When I realized she was never writing about the details of what was done, that she was talking from voices through stories & glimpses and experiences. It was like seeing a journey in the pain that could be equally and truthfully explored. So many of the poems are titled with Cree and an English sort of translation. I grieve, I felt it, without the story telling me why she was hurting.

Carla shared one more thing over a coffee. People going through these kinds of experiences often make "being done with it" their goal. The lesson she learned was to see this kind of pain as part of her. Which gave her control over it. Perhaps this is a more realistic description of how art works: it takes the thing inside us and makes it visible—no longer the monster we believe is there but can't see.

How many people, Indigenous or not (like Carla), have been saved or helped to find their way by a poem or story or song? Sometimes it happens in a decisive moment as it did for Bill Murray in his *Song of the Lark* story—the painting he talks about. For most it takes time and as much effort as the creation of the work itself, with layers and resonances that only become apparent afterward.

It would be a failure for a book or painting to simply describe the darkness, the outright crimes and cruelties humans visit on each other, illness, dysfunction, weaknesses, and sorrow. There has to be more to life than simply surviving. For, as the late Harold Johnson (Woodland Cree) said, if we only have one story—one of victimhood, and ourselves as fractured people in fractured communities—that is the story we become. My friend doesn't look away from what happened, she simply refuses to allow it to define her. While facing one kind of past, Louise Bernice Halfe – Sky Dancer's stories also celebrate the grandmothers, family, resilience, spirit and traditional knowledge, love, sex, and a good time. Even in difficult work like hers, beauty takes a deep path into ourselves. It takes us to the extreme edge of what art can do, even when the idea of saving another person is the furthest thing from the mind of the poet, painter, or the musician in her makeshift studio. I'm not sure there will ever be a compelling explanation of how this happens. After twenty years I can still hear Chick Harrity telling his story of little Nhanny in that shed of his. I remember the beat-up binder and how he protected it, the image turned slightly toward me. I can't seem to let it go, nor do I want to. To these friends, I offer my own dedication.

DEDICATION

to the fierceness of nothing left, to silence
and simply coming through; dedication to our own breath now
and what we make of it, beauty a kind of resistance
because it isn't expected from the likes of us. This is for names
untranslatable, Sky Dancer, a gift she says. For my friend
writing and recovering, then writing more. This is the solace
of quiet halls, a painted field at dawn and the bird
we're only told is there as its song
opens a doorway in the side of the mind.

This is for the concert crowd on the grass, the shimmer
of evening and the parable of a slowly strummed heart as love
gets older without letting go. Dedication to nothing heroic,
to what we save without knowing, the photographer
with Saigon thirty years in his mind—the impatient taxi
and the box on the sidewalk barely holding itself together
as the girl inside sleeps, and what makes him tell the taxi to stop.
This is for love poems and every poem ever smuggled.
This for a girl barefoot among cables, looping a guitar riff, who
says music saved her, or maybe believing music could do that
is really what saved her. May we believe too.
Dedication to the light that finds its way out of us,
to beauty which endures, and outlives us all.

PART 4

Buzzy the Kamikaze Rabbit

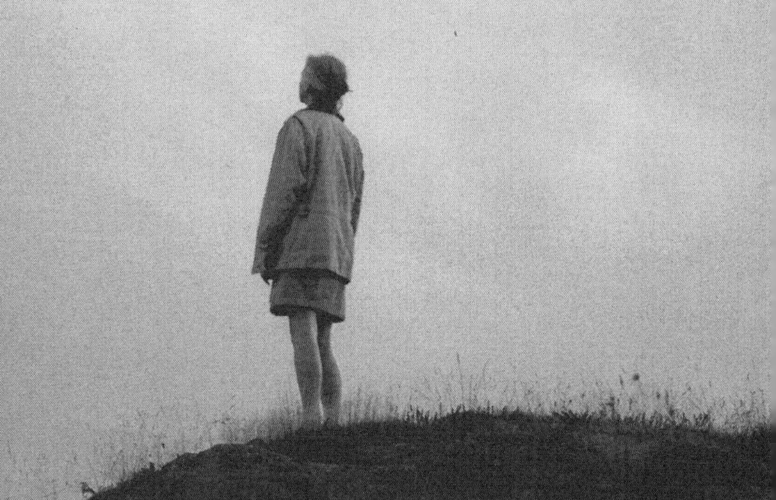

DARTMOUTH, NOVA SCOTIA, 1974

Maybe it's me or maybe it's my sister Jen—the way we seem to live one notice away from eviction. Two months ago, she brought home a juvenile liver-spotted rabbit she calls Buzzy. He's putting on weight and has started to look like my brother-in-law. The windows in our third-floor apartment rattle from November to March as the draft blows the curtains six inches out from the sill. If we're going to be evicted from our Tulip Street Hilton because of the wildlife, why not a dog or a cat? Compared with the inertia of a rabbit, the straight-shooting ingratitude of a cat is positively refreshing. The bush rabbits my brothers hunted when I was a kid wound up as pelts that dried out like shingles tacked to the rafters above our room in the basement. Their demise didn't bother us. You don't have to be very bright to be someone's lunch. The elusive jackrabbit, of course, is in a different league. It's actually a hare, and its life is a race from start to finish. A jackrabbit's legs are like pistons that leave no doubt what they're for: fight or flight. On the Autobahn of evolution, the sluggish domestic rabbit is an offence to natural science.

* * *

Jen has somehow failed to notice that rabbits eat their environment: wood, potted plants, books left on the floor, slippers. Everything. Their incisors need exercise. Why settle for alfalfa pellets when you live in a greasy spoon diner? Buzzy eschews baseboards and moulding in favour of spruce cupboard doors, which crunch up nicely. Any kid who has tasted a piece of second-hand furniture knows that varnish has a sweet, yet pleasantly salty taste. To Buzzy, it's like honey glaze on a beer nut—pure MSG.

Jen says it's cruel to keep a rabbit in a cage, so she locks him in the bathroom while we're at work. The first time she did it, Buzzy shredded a whole roll of toilet paper until it covered the floor like tickertape. The next day she put him in the bathtub. He was still there when we got home, reared back on his hind legs, in the centre of a halo of chunky blue confetti that used to be our bath mat. I'm sure he resents us for making him spend all day in solitary. Perhaps celibacy is getting to him the way it gets to all teenagers, but he seems to avoid us, me in particular, and in his own dim-witted way he seems anxious. Jumpy.

Two weeks ago, I came home from another day of painting old peoples' houses, cleaning their windows, and stripping seven years' worth of paste wax from chipped linoleum floors—all the jobs that a BA in psychology so usefully prepared me for. I was in a hurry to use the can, which is why I opened the bathroom door so abruptly. Buzzy was perched on the sill of the open window. He immediately stopped nibbling the lead-based paint, took one startled look at me, then his two huge glutei maximi launched him into the wild blue yonder like a cotton ball with afterburners. His flattened, furry corpse was nowhere to be seen on the ground below. I raced down to the backyard, a waist-high no man's land of thistles, half-buried cinder blocks, and rusty chicken wire. I was pretty sure the rotting fence was enough to stop a rabbit with a concussion, but still—no Buzzy.

I looked up at the peeling, battleship grey wall of the building. It slowly dawned on me that a miracle had occurred. Buzzy had gone sideways and crash-landed on the balcony of the apartment below us. Whatever the bone-crunching fall had done, Buzzy was alive. Our second-floor neighbour, Bill, is an alcoholic. Fragments of his life waft upward through our windows. We hear table legs scrape the floor, muffled voices, or a crash followed by a few seconds of shuffling. Nothing alarming. He must hear us too; he must know our footsteps, where we will go before we get there, our thumps and patterns. I went back inside and knocked on his door.

"Bill, are you in?" There was no answer, so I turned the knob and walked in. I called again, then headed for the sliding door of the balcony. There was Bill, too hammered to get up. He wore a Hawaiian shirt with a pineapple motif and flashes of the Pacific in the background. A half-finished mug of Captain Morgan rum tilted forward in his right hand. He was bracing himself against the back of his lawn chair as he focused on something straight ahead. He was eye-to-bleary-eye with the six-pound liver-spotted rabbit that dropped from the sky a few minutes ago. Buzzy had apparently landed on the chair facing him. Bill seemed relieved to see me and offered me a drink, a non-alien that could speak without moving its nose. Buzzy just sat there as if nothing had happened.

* * *

Buzzy the Kamikaze Rabbit has flown again. I went into the bathroom two nights ago. Buzzy was back on the window ledge taking in the thunderstorm and the rush of rain through the trees. I don't know why a door latch should startle him more than fork lightning, but he gave me that look I'd seen once before and simply vanished into the wall of black. I ran down the stairs, with Jen close behind me this time. Buzzy was splayed out on the ground. I could almost see a small ring of blue birds tweeting as they circled his head. It was like Looney Tunes gone documentary. I skied toward him on the greasy muck, but as soon as he saw me he started to crawl into the narrow gap below the main-floor balcony. I tried not to think about what the neighbourhood cats had deposited in there as I wormed my way in after him. When I finally managed to corner him, he let fly with a half-hearted rabbit punch, then gave up. He seemed depressed more than anything.

I was still covered in muck when Jen and I climbed into a cab with our patient between us in an apple box. The driver eyed us suspiciously in the mirror all the way to the twenty-four-hour animal clinic. The place was empty except for us. The young vet took her time gingerly raising Buzzy up by the stomach, pulling back his gums to study the teeth and tongue, and looking into both red eyes with a light. She inserted a needle into a bottle and administered a shot. Half a day's pay later she gave us the news: Buzzy had a broken tooth that would grow back in no time.

* * *

Creatures like Buzzy have a way of making stories happen. My hair is silver and quite fine these days. Not the mopey, nondescript shag I used to have. "Buzzy" is hard to forget. I have to wonder why humans can't see these train wrecks coming. Rabbits belong in the bush with owls and hawks, and where they have real camouflage instead of the cheap plush pet rabbits share with couches from Uneeda Discount and tea box bestiaries of monkeys and ceramic owls presided over by perpetually dipping storks with cherry red bulbs for an ass. I get the feeling our pets are trying to send us a message. They use the same macabre signals they have been trying to teach us for years. I got a letter from my six-year-old niece:

Dear Uncle Bruce and Aunt Joanne
I had a good Christmas did you?
I got two goldfish for Christmas but one died.
I named them Bruce and Joanne.
The goldfish that died was named Bruce.

Rabbits and cats finish their allotted span out in the yard pushing up quack grass. Goldfish are buried at sea. I can still see the way Buzzy looked straight at me just before he jumped. Was it panic or just exasperation beyond endurance, as if I'm the one who can't get the point? For every pet disaster there's a human one just as stupid and just as inevitable. Our minds lurch into gear for the fiftieth time, as we crash into our fate. We never seem to learn the lesson.

* * *

I was lined up at the bar at a family wedding in Goose Bay, Labrador, when I met a man who had been drinking out for weeks on the story that he had recently been hit by lightning. It seemed to have left him with a bottomless thirst. The fellow described in slurred Labradorean dialect how he and one of his buddies built a hunting shack out in the boonies. They slapped it together with plywood and galvanized nails. They added a cast iron stove with a pipe hooked up through the roof. He was quite proud and particular about the fact that they saved themselves the trip to town by liberating railroad ties from a handy pile they found by the train track. The ties made perfect floor joists. It never registered that they had built a lightning rod the size of a summer kitchen on treeless, flat terrain in the middle of one of the most lightning-prone regions in Canada. When the inevitable happened, the air started to crackle. A blinding flash tossed him over top of the stove and slapped his buddy against the opposite wall like an X-ray. "I could see the bones in his arms," the man at the bar said.

The story left a trail of dots that my new friend still couldn't connect. I suspect there is a recessive lightning gene. Some people are hit by high voltage before they are born and spend the rest of their lives waiting for the visual effects to catch up. We all have our blind spots. We are attracted to our own demise like an addiction we can't be warned off of. Afternoon reality shows fill their lineups with women who are attracted to terrible men—rounders and felons. But how many men can honestly say that the biggest mistake in their life wasn't lit up like Ringling Brothers Circus. The Buzzys of this world know a lot about fate and how stupid it is. Philosophers debate free will and whether there exists in our nature some unchangeable fact, an irreducible part of us that can't be altered except by annihilation: a place without windows. All we can do is hope for the best and carry on, oblivious to things we can't avoid because they are part of us. We walk into rooms without thinking. We load our pockets with nails, then walk out onto the treeless landscape and wait like a post for the lighting we know will come. Our pets understand we can't help it.

PART 5

Silence, A Brother's Journal

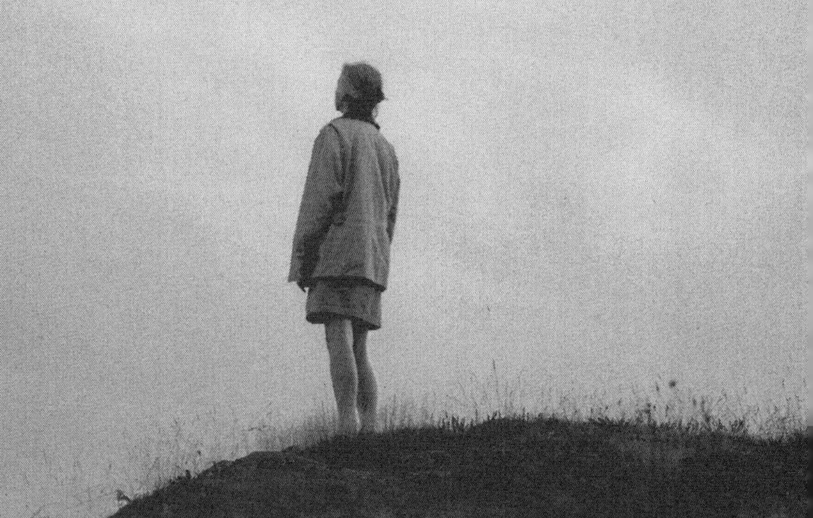

MAY 1

10:45 PM. Dartmouth General Hospital.
Lights dim. Oxygen at 80 percent. The hubbub's died down. I drove my sisters Jen and Maureen home earlier tonight. I'm back at the ICU for the late evening watch. Our older sister, Anne, lies quietly. Jen is the only one in the family who is fluent in American Sign Language, or ASL. She signed, *I love you, Anne,* before they put our deaf sister under the anesthetic so they could hook up the ventilator, the letters *I* and *L* formed together, as her hand waved to the right. It's the same sign we now press against Anne's warm belly as her diaphragm heaves. Respiration 27 breaths per minute. Heart 92. Perspiration soaks her thin brown hair and forms a fine mist on her forehead.

The doctor describes the downward trend and the sixteen-year-old who lasted like this for three weeks. The lights are low. A blue computer screen casts its signature inside the nurses' station in the middle of the ward. An array of small white monitors hangs from the gurneys on both sides of Anne's bed. The defibrillator paddles and valves for oxygen are set into the wall behind her head. The bed is equipped with a warm bladder that molds to Anne's body, imperceptibly tilting a few degrees on one side, sending small pulses to massage her and stimulate circulation after three days of immobility. I wonder what Anne makes of it. We used to be able to wake her up by standing outside her door and stamping on the floor so she could feel the vibrations coming up through the bedpost. It's impressive in such a small hospital, but there is also some truth behind the cliché—what all this paraphernalia stands for: counterfeit hope, the sedative of science.

It took Maureen and me eight hours to get here from Saskatchewan, flying Air Canada. She lives on a 110-acre farm, a "small quarter" big enough for my brother-in-law to raise and break horses when he's not at his day job. Mo used to work ambulances, but now she has a business teaching first aid. She has seen a lot in the back of ambulances. She knows the machines, who's likely to make it no matter how messed up they are, and how others slip away when no one is watching. She is stocky and four foot ten in her socks. One could mistake her for Anne if not for Mo's short, strawberry-blond hair and the way she snaps back with a zinger, a habit you get when you're married to a practical joker for twenty-six years.

The ICU nurse says Anne has one of the fastest progressing cases of bacterial pneumonia they have ever seen. Her temperature has been over 40

(104°F), and they are trying to bring it down without much success. I know this malevolent shade. It was the raging fever from spinal meningitis that destroyed Anne's hearing. The truth is my sister isn't expected to make it through another night, maybe two at the most. I have come for Jen as much as for Anne. Jen has translated and run interference with Anne's doctors and social workers, hospitals and group homes all these years. Her words come out in a flurry, and after so many years Down East she has a stronger Nova Scotian accent than her kids who were born here. None of us are saints, but so much has fallen to Jen, the only one in the family living here on the coast with Anne.

I never learned to sign and have a hard time reading the finger spelling. Like French, it's easier to speak than to understand if there's no one to practise with. The experts and books all said that a child who signs would not be motivated to learn to speak, and my parents believed them. You can get used to not hearing, but a child could have told them: there is more than one kind of silence. Now every sentence is a strain. Because of language, there are simple things that Anne and I will never be able to say. Tonight, my fingers wrap around hers. I press them into her palm, forming the letter *U*.

It's strangely familiar how all this feels: the watching, the way we circle each other like moons. There are such things in the universe, the existence of objects known only by the effects of their gravity. I see her shadows, the small dry lake in the corner of her eye, where two days ago a few tears trickled out of her. Anne's heart rate is 91. It should be 70. Respiration 24. It has been over 30, which is almost double what it would be if her lungs were working.

MAY 2

2:15 PM

Rest. Hope again. I leave ICU for a break. I lived in the Maritimes for ten years. The jobs were precarious, including my time at a Dartmouth Boys and Girls Club, a temporary place run out of the dingy basement of St. Anthony's Church. The public housing across the street was built next to the lines from the coal-fired power plant. I liked the kids and I liked walking to work along Windmill Road with its glimpses of the grey, working harbour. I heard more music played at house parties in my first year in Nova Scotia than I had in my entire life until then—a mélange of Cape Breton fiddle tunes, a guitar or piano laying down chords, dark rum, John Prine, spirituals, the Stones, and *You Are My Sunshine* more times than I can count. I took drawing classes and finally finished my degree in this clannish, best, and most familiar place.

I call Saskatchewan from the deck of the Dartmouth ferry. No answer. There's a hockey game on TV in the Irish pub on the Halifax side. This is as far as I'll go. *Canada 4, Sweden 2*. Anne is half an hour away, and I wonder if I'm too far from the hospital if anything happens. Most of the tables are still empty. The waitress says there won't be any deep-fried clams until Friday since the season has just started. It used to be poor man's food, but tourists in souvenir sweaters strolling the dock-side shops on Privateers' Wharf crave it, the rustic fare of what the brochures refer to as "authentic sea and shore," as if one can tell what is true and what is not by the taste.

The last time I was here, Anne treated me to supper, a mixed platter of clams, scallops, and mussels. Or maybe this is me inventing again: the food, and my kids happy for once on the vacation they mostly resented. Three sails wave *L. L. L.* on the tall ship from some university, out in the harbour. The sun dips behind the stone walls of the Citadel, the British fort overlooking the streets running down to the port. A few steady lights illuminate the newly painted freighter that sits at anchor off McNabs Island. Her crew watches for what comes out of the channel, from the deep part of the water.

11:20 PM

Jen and Mo have gone home. Just now in the waiting room I was speaking with Susan, who lives in Lunenburg County. She came in with pains in both arms. The EMTs gave her something she calls "B-blockers," which probably saved her life. We talk about the old stores downtown, *Uneeda Discount*, and laugh. She went to the old LaHave school fifty years ago, the same place Jen lived in for a while when I was still Down East. Susan wonders if I knew a girl named Spearwater from some place down the road that ended in *River.*

I used to be able to tell where people were from by the way they talked, Bridgewater being different from LaHave or Mahone Bay. Susan's married daughter lives in Birmingham, where she has picked up an Alabama accent and writes letters home filled with *you-all's.* My friends back in Regina think I'm from here, maybe because of the way I lay on my vowels or drop them completely from the first half of a compound word, *N'brunsw'k.* It is not as though I have abandoned the language, but it fades deeper into my memory, the way fish swim through stone until their eyes turn dusty and their bones fall to the bottom of the limestone sea.

11:40 PM. Oxygen reduced to 60 percent. Respiration still at 27.
I explain to the new nurse that Anne has almost 100 percent hearing loss, and we are here so she knows she isn't alone. The nurse replies my sister will remember none of this. Even people in a coma remember voices, so why not a hand brushing an arm if touch is how we speak? Anne has taught touch-sign to deaf-blind people. If we stop, what will happen to the language we make now, the signs forgotten, like the accents of those villages along the South Shore after the children disappear into gated communities down in the States or they fly to the prairies like me? Even now, as I think this, I can see how this place took me into itself and became part of my restlessness.

I'm taking a chance turning the reading lamp on so I can see this page. Anne's heart rate increases when they adjust the tubes or wash her. Her breathing gets shallow and her oxygen drops. She knows things are happening. Perhaps she knows this light is my light. My left hand holds hers as I write, balancing the pad precariously on my knee, as if the letters could travel up my arm, across my shoulders and down again, finding my fingertips, barely more than a whisper at the edge of my skin.

On behalf of the sleeper I would like to say
the fish is aware of the sea.

MAY 3, MAY 4

Two lost days. What happened? Perhaps I'll remember later.

MAY 5

12:35 AM

I went out with Jen and Mo last night. But Anne has been in ICU for seven days and things may go no further. Her lungs look like a white shroud in the X-rays. The doctors and nurses have started to set us up for "the talk." They act as if we're so dense we don't see it coming. My sister has beaten the odds so far. Her organs didn't bleed, one of the deadly side-effects of a last-ditch treatment—an enzyme that kills the bacteria causing the pneumonia. It costs $12,000 for a course of treatment lasting a day. *Thank you, Medicare.* Doctors returning for the mid-week shift are surprised to see she is "still here." By which, of course, they mean not dead. There is grim satisfaction in this, but it will mean nothing if they can't get her off the respirator. Her lungs need to push air by themselves. With all her systems working, it could come to weeks or months under sedation, hooked up to the machine and waiting for a blood clot, for an opportunistic infection, or for fluid on her heart to finish the job.

Today Mo said it too. "It could all mean nothing," she said. "This bug doesn't care." And there it is, formed in our minds. The pneumonia is no longer a colony, a nasty bacterium, but a thing with a will that has inserted itself into our lives: not malevolent, but simply indifferent.

1:30 PM

The South African doctor is hopeful. The X-rays continue to clear and two units of blood have been ordered. Anne needs hemoglobin to fix more oxygen in her blood stream and to get her blood oxygen count out of the sixties. They're getting ready for a tracheostomy—to put a breathing tube in her throat—and want her in the best shape possible. They wouldn't do this if they didn't think she had a chance. Some of these doctors are optimistic by nature and some have learned not to be. Their actions are clear enough. A few days ago, they were talking about "decisions" that will have to be made if she crashes. The next unspoken question, what if they can't get her off the respirator? Here come the euphemisms again: about what to do with our sister, age 56 years and 10 months, heavily sedated and expected to remain so, heart beating, kidneys healthy, brain (so far as can be determined) working. Even now, if they reduced the sedation she would be strong enough to try to pull the tubes out of her arms and throat, fully aware of her own panic, the doctors, and us. They'd have to sedate her again. Being strong or scared doesn't matter. This bug doesn't care.

MAY 7

1:54 PM

This morning Jen's husband and I took the old road to Bridgewater to visit his son. It's the first sunny day in a week and I need to get out of town. Jen and Mo have been at the hospital all day. The nurses say they have to make a decision tomorrow. What they mean isn't clear. But Anne has been on the respirator for ten days and it looks like we've hit a wall. She still isn't well enough to get onto a trach tube. This morning Anne's eyes were partly open—the first time we have seen them in a week. My sister Jen frantically tried to sign to her and called out *Anne, Anne.* We had to calm her down since Anne cannot see any of this and any disturbance sends her vitals spiraling. Her eyes are grey-blue like my father's. They're almost opaque, with no light in them, and yet an eyelid flickers. The nurse says that earlier one of the staff from the group home signed using touch-sign for the deaf-blind and Anne responded.

MAY 8

12:55 PM. Written from memory, no place or time to write.
Sometime this morning they adjusted the respirator to see if Anne can take some breaths on her own. The machine is now assisting rather than breathing for her. It is the first real sign she may be able to get off it, perhaps as soon as Thursday, two days from now. Her sedation has been reduced and her eyes open briefly—long enough for Jen to sign *You have been very, very sick* (fingers of both hands making twin Vs that are touched together; the sign for *sick* is middle finger of left hand touched to forehead, middle finger of right hand touched to chest).

Sometimes while we are at her bedside or when I am milling around, I feel suddenly weepy. Mo and I walk down the block to John's Lunch after our turn at the hospital, Mo orders a BLT and I get a plate of deep-fried clams. I've been craving them since I got here. Comfort food. After a while I realize neither of us have been speaking. We have simply been staring at our own plates and thinking. The good news is almost as hard to take as the bad. It leaves me out of place as if the last ten days belong to a stranger.

MAY 9

1:05 PM

Anne's blood oxygen is still at 40 percent, the mark needed to get her off the respirator. We weren't here this morning when they cut the sedative to encourage her to do more breathing on her own. They tell us she was lucid, and very anxious like everyone who wakes up on a respirator. Jen tries signing when Anne's eyes open, but we don't know how much she sees. Jen teaches Mo and me signs: both hands held to the chest as we mimic the act of inhaling. Hands held apart and gesturing wider, meaning *Bigger. Bigger breaths. Slowly.*

And that's what Anne does. Her body heaves and the wave on the machine leaps, the small mountain squared off at the top before it drops off, a short space as it starts again, breaking the steady pattern of small hills when the respirator takes over. I wonder if this is doing any good, but her respiration rate settles down and the machine shows that she has taken a few deep breaths. The main thing is she is better than yesterday. We hope the staff believe us when we tell them she's responding to our signs. I can see it in some of them. Meanings felt like gentle pressures over great distances. A few more fish in the sea.

9:10 PM

They just increased the sedative so Anne can sleep. One of us will come back at 6:30 AM so we can be here when she comes out of it. Her breathing is rough—frequent and shallow rather than regular and deep like it needs to be. I hold her right hand and make the sign for "slow." My fingers rest over the back of hers then I brush upward toward her wrist, which is how the sign would feel if she made it herself. This was Mo's discovery earlier this afternoon. Here we are as if we were kids again, improvising a language, but now it's more urgent.

9:30 PM. Respiration 25. Less than half of the breaths belong to Anne.

Anne seems to be watching me with one eye open. Her body heaves as if she is trying to cough. I'm still not used to this even though there's no cause for alarm. Is she watching me writing? Does she think it's a dream: her brother appears out of a fog from two thousand miles away and suddenly knows how to sign. The nurse hears the beep, tries to suction. She opens the valve that increases the sedative.

MAY 12

10:30 PM
Another rough night. About 4:00 AM my sister's respiration rate and blood pressure shot way up. It was pretty serious and they had to do a lot of work to get things under control. The blood pressure was still high but coming down when Jen arrived this morning. Right now, everything seems to be under control. The pneumonia is clearing, but Anne's lungs have fluid in them, which was probably what brought on the trouble last night. The good news is that while changing the tubes today, the nurse disconnected the sedative by accident. People come out of it very quickly, which is what Anne did. Her first words were: *What the hell is going on?* Then she repeated it. Everybody, including the nurse and respirologist cracked up. No one could believe it.

They turned the sedative off and Anne seems to tolerate the trach tube pretty well. She has been reading our signs and responding to messages on the white board. She was still lucid this evening. The fact we can communicate with her means we can give her instructions about her breathing and she can tell us if she is having any discomfort. We have arranged interpreter service so that the medical staff can communicate directly with Anne, who hates talking to others through us, especially Jen.

Mo flew home today. There is nothing like having your personal EMT on-call. She has been a terrific help and can kick butt when needed. As we walked to John's Lunch the other day, she said, almost matter-of-factly, that all of this will change our lives. I feel it too, the beginning of a trajectory, something ahead pulling us toward it. I can't make it out. In the meantime, we try to keep ourselves together. I will miss her.

MAY 15

3:30 PM
Two lost days. Yesterday and the day before tangle together. Today is already shrouding over. From memory then:

Mother's Day, May 13th
I slip away from the house early to buy Mother's Day cards for Jen and Anne. I'm surprised by the number of people picking through the leftover cards halfway through the morning. Perhaps they're on their way to see their mothers over the bridge in Halifax. Anne is awake when I get to the ward. Her eyes open wide, and I realize how difficult this is going to be. I sign a few words. Anne is on light sedation. She had a turn during the night and has fluid in her lungs. The doctor says that she could have had a mild heart failure. She's stable now and he seems content to wait until Monday for an echocardiogram.

I sign *Hi Anne,* and she mouths *Hello.* I put her glasses on her face and hold up the card for her to read. I tell her that Mo has gone home and Jen is sleeping in. I struggle through the one-way conversation. When I get back to Jen's, I take a taxi to the Halifax ferry and wander the old streets near the water. I'm surprised the shops are open this early in the season. The chill stabs through my thin summer jacket and worries my bones. The world seems to be leaving me further and further behind.

May 14, 2:00 PM
Frances, the sign interpreter Jen and I have requested, meets us beside Anne's bed. We call the doctor over. Frances is the hearing child of two deaf parents. Sometime over the next couple of days she tells me that she always resented being a go-between who signed for her parents for hearing people. She says that the day she refused to sign for them and started just being their daughter their lives got better. Anne's deaf friends know she's in ICU. This is my sister's world. Like always, I don't know them and they don't know me. For now, they only have fragments and rumours.

I'm surprised by this doctor's bluntness. He doesn't have a bedside manner and knows it. He talks as if there is as stopwatch ticking away in his pocket. The first thing he tells Anne is that she has been very, very sick. Next, he says she had to be put on "a machine to help her breathe" as if she doesn't know what a respirator is. He says she has been here for three weeks. I think this is wrong but realize, yes, her first visit to Emergency, when they sent her home with antibiotics, was three weeks ago today. This finally seems to hit her—how sick she has been. He says it is important for her to breathe slowly and deeply. That seems to be it. He has told us nothing. The doctor leaves and we stay. I use the interpreter a few times instead of relying on Jen, my own speech and finger spelling, or the whiteboard. But most of the time, I stay at the end of the bed.

Jen and I go for lunch. I do some errands and drive her back to the hospital, then leave. Anne is distressed when Jen and I return in the afternoon. She believes she is going to die. We try to explain that she's getting better, but she doesn't believe us.

Today, 6:10 PM. Heart rate 124. Respiration 38.
I come to the hospital right after supper. I want a few minutes alone with Anne before I leave tomorrow. I'm surprised to see her turned on her side. Her face is flushed and her temperature has been between 39 and 40 degrees, where it was when I saw her on the first Saturday. Earlier today the doctor said she may have a recurrence of the pneumonia or perhaps a second case of hospital-induced pneumonia from being immobilized and on the respirator for so long. They have given her a stronger antibiotic and are testing her blood. Anne seems distant. Her eyes barely open. She tries to mouth a few words. I rinse out a cloth with cold water from the sink at the nurse's station and put it on her forehead. I show her the get-well card made by Jen's granddaughter.

Emily has drawn a card with hearts and flowers, and a picture of Anne on a bed. The four legs are sprawled out at angles like matchsticks. She has drawn Anne's hair and face with yellow markers. Red for the body. The woman in the bed is smiling. Anne looks at the card as I hold it up, but she doesn't respond. I tell her I am flying home to Regina tomorrow. She doesn't respond to this either. Her eyes are half open. I turn down the nurse's offer of a stool and stand by her bed another twenty minutes. Anne's eyes close. She may be sleeping, but sometimes she does this when she wants you to leave or doesn't want a conversation. I stay a while longer. Her eyes open just as I'm about to leave. I pull one strap of my knapsack over my shoulder and wave goodbye. The bed is too high and too wide to give her a hug with all the equipment in the way. So I sign, *I love you,* a new sign I have learned in the conversation around the bed, then head out past the nurses' station.

I stop to thank them and to tell them I am heading back to Regina tomorrow. One of them tells me she thought I was from here, which, if you know Nova Scotians, is a compliment.

MAY 16

I wake up at 4:30 AM. I brush my teeth and shave before I realize I'm up an hour early. I go back to bed and get up again when I hear my brother-in-law stirring in the next room. I dress quickly while he showers and stick my head in Jen's room to let her know I am leaving. She hasn't been asleep for long, a couple of hours at the most. I put my duffel bag and knapsack by the door. We don't say much. A few sentences. She thanks me for coming.

It's barely light as I drive to the airport. I turn onto the overpass built over the spot where there used to be a roundabout with roads spinning off in four directions. The drive to the airport seems shorter than I remember, but of course it must be the same. I pass a string of lakes I never visited when I lived here. I didn't have a car back then and never seemed to have the time. Two weeks ago, sitting by Anne's bed, time was the silent friend. Passing time meant hope, the slowing of Death's march toward us. But looking at these lakes now, bulldozers scraping forest and fragile layers of earth from hilltops to make way for condominiums and shopping centres, I feel that something decent and good has been lost. I come to the crest of a low hill. I always knew I was on my way home when I reached the top—the muted sky, black spruce looming, and the road rolling empty before me like an Alex Colville painting where the eye follows the path of light through the dusky land, all the way to the vanishing point.

They still haven't found the reason for Anne's fever, which should be gone by now. There will be a long struggle ahead. If the pneumonia doesn't beat her, she could have up to a year of rehabilitation. I try not to think about it. I have made no promises, no resolutions. The light is too fragile. I have done too little and I have nothing to swear by, but this isn't what I want to leave in my journal so instead I write:

I will swear by love, how it stood in the room, its shadow
*marking the hours so we wouldn't have to.**

---

* Note to the reader: Anne survived the pneumonia, albeit with some lasting challenges, and was able to return home.

Acknowledgements

I gratefully acknowledge the people and organizations whose help, generosity, and time has made this journey possible. As I mentioned previously, any fault is my own. I would like to acknowledge organizations like Ohio History Connection and Indigenous peoples working to preserve and honour the ceremonial sites of the Ohio River Valley. A group of these sites, including those appearing here, received a UNESCO World Heritage Site designation in 2023. Huge thanks to the Greater Cincinnati Native American Coalition for the welcome and the opportunity to participate in four days of ceremony and sharing at the World Day of Prayer and Peace at Fort Ancient, Ohio. I'm grateful to Knowledge Keeper Joseph Naytowhow (Cree) for conversation and advice on the Hopewell Earthworks section, and much more. So much has been added by permission to quote from Margaret Wickens Pearce's (Potawatomi) paper on mapping; Tim Chilcott's wonderful translation of Matsuo Bashō's famous work, *The Narrow Road to the Deep North*; and Timothy Al Price, who had a good chuckle with the poetic license taken with his paper on the Great Hopewell Road. Special thanks to the family of little Noah, in "Remembering and Forgetting." Noah is not forgotten. The Indigenous peoples historically occupying or claiming land in Ohio include the Shawnee, Ojibwa, Delaware, Wyandotte, Eel River, Kaskaskia, Haudenosaunee, Miami, Munsee, Seneca-Cayuga, Ottawa, Piankashaw, Sauk, Potawatomi, Seneca, and Wea peoples.

The excerpt of the Jerry Rush poem, "After Reading 'Madrigal' by Felix Grande," in the Little Voices section is from *The Bones of Their Occasion* (Cormorant Books). Thanks as well to Louise Bernice Halfe – Sky Dancer (Cree) for the lines from her poem "Dedication to the Seventh Generation" from *Burning in This Midnight Dream* (Coteau Books, 2016) and to Regina writer Carla Harris, who lends her own words to "Song of the Lark." "Silence, A Brother's Journal" appeared in Issue 91.2 of *The Dalhousie Review*.

I would especially like to thank Brian Bartlett, my editor, who brought generosity, and a keen eye and ear to the prose and poetry. Duncan Noel Campbell and Kelly Laycock, the designer and the copy editor, helped to bring a sense of form, wholeness, and precision to a sometimes challenging book. SK Arts and Access Copyright Foundation provided support for travel to Ohio on this project. The generous advice and encouragement of Regina's Radiant Press through the evolution of this project is greatly appreciated. As always, thanks to my fellow members of The Poets Combine for their keen eyes and fellowship. We especially honour the memory and legacy of Combine member Byrna Barclay, whose spirit, love of the art, and endless generosity to writers and writing in this province continues to touch those who will never meet her.

Notes

FOREWORD

1 In Japanese, there is no exact word for a poetic journal. The word *utanikki* has been used by some scholars and Canadian poet Fred Wah in *So Far* (Talon Books, 1991). Wah's book includes "Limestone Lakes Utaniki" (an alternate spelling), "Uluru Utaniki," and "Dead in My Tracks: Wildcat Creek Utaniki."

2 Greg Johnson, "Caring for Depressed Cultural Sites, Hawaiian Style," in Lindsay Jones and Richard D. Shields, eds., *The Newark Earthworks: Enduring Monuments, Contested Meanings* (University of Virginia Press, 2016), p. 262–76.

PART 1: HOPEWELL EARTHWORKS DAYBOOK

1 Arrival, Columbus, Ohio. "Hold on to a peg...," is found text used with permission from Margaret Wickens Pierce, "The Cartographic Legacy of the Newark Earthworks," in Lindsay Jones and Richard D. Shields, eds., *The Newark Earthworks: Enduring Monuments, Contested Meanings* (University of Virginia Press, 2016), 188.

2 The Matsuo Bashō quotes are cited with permission. Matsuo Bashō, *The Narrow Road to the Deep North, trans.* Tim Chilcott (Tim Chilcott Literary Translations, 2004), 6–7, 38–39, http://www.tclt.org.uk/basho/Oku_2011.pdf.

3 Columbus to Peebles, and the Great Serpent Mound. A telling of the Corn Mother legend may be found in Richard Erdoes and Alfonso Otiz, eds., *American Indian Myths and Legends* (New York: Pantheon Books, 1984), 11–13. The story here is also from correspondence with Knowledge Keeper Joseph Naytowhow (Cree).

4 Great Serpent Mound age. While the site includes an Adena burial mound (about 300 BCE), Brad Lepper, curator of archaeology for the Ohio History Connection, and other colleagues believe the Serpent Mound was created by the Fort Ancient people around 1170. This is based on the prominence of the Serpent in the Fort Ancient and Mississippian culture, and its prominence in other sites and artifacts of this later period. While this seems to be the dominant attribution, other writers cite carbon dating and the importance of the serpent in earlier cultures. The debate continues.

5 The First Heavy Metal Church of Christ, Dayton, OH, accessed 2017, https://www.heavymetalchurch.com/.

6 Remembering and Forgetting. In addition to Dr. Robin Fleming's research, support for the idea of revered child burials in ancient Britain is from Bradford Brickman, "'Most Innocent, Most Happy, Most Dear': Child Burials in Roman Britain," *Bradford unconsidered trifles* (blog), January 19, 2026, https://bradfordunconsideredtrifles.wordpress.com/2016/01/19.

7 Remembering and Forgetting. Statements on the fate of children in Canada's Indian residential schools are from the Truth and Reconciliation Commission of Canada's final report. Justice Murray Sinclair, Chair of the TRC, estimates that 25,000 to 30,000 children died while in the "care" of Canada's Indian residential schools. The equation given later in the section for children lost at the Regina Indian Industrial School is known as PYLL, or Potential Years of Life Lost. It measures the impact of mortality at a younger age than expected due to illness or other causes in a population. The estimated 1748 years PYLL at RIIS is the author's calculation. According to the TRC, tuberculosis was the greatest single cause of such deaths. British Columbia and Saskatchewan had the highest number of documented residential school deaths of all Canadian provinces, but those recorded deaths are a fraction of the total.

8 Noah's story and poem are presented with permission of the family.

9 William F. Romaine and Jarrod Burks, "LiDAR Imaging of the Great Hopewell Road," Ohio Archaeological Council, February 2008. Accessed June 24, 2024, https://www.academia.edu/24034721/LiDAR_Imaging_of_the_Great_Hopewell_Road.

10 Wickens Pearce, "The Cartographic Legacy of the Newark Earthworks," 190.

11 Timothy A. Price, "The Great Hopewell Road: GIS Solutions Toward Pathway Discovery," *Hopewell Archaeology: The Newsletter of Hopewell Archaeology in the Ohio River Valley* 7, no. 1 (December 2006). GIS (Geographic Information Systems) is a powerful system of creating digital maps that incorporate multiple layers of boundaries, images, natural and man-made features, and data. In this case, remnants of the old road, elevations, land cover, and other features were used to determine the most likely route of the road.

12 Caution to the golfer. Cited from Benjamin J. Barnes (Second Chief, Shawnee Tribe), "Becoming Our Own Storytellers: Tribal Nations Engaging with Academia," in Stephen Warren, ed., *The Eastern Shawnee Tribe of Oklahoma: Resilience through Adversity* (Norman: University of Oklahoma Press, 2017). The last sentence is a poetic embellishment by the author.

13 The land where the Octagon and Circle is located was originally leased from the City of Newark in 1910. The site is now owned by the Ohio History Connection. A group of these sites received a UNESCO World Heritage designation in 2023. At the time of this publication a process is underway to compensate and remove the current tenant, the

Mound Builders Country Club, from the Octagon and Circle, which will then become a publicly accessible historic park.

14 Tim Jordan, site manager of Flint Ridge Memorial State Park, Glenford, OH, at the time of the author's visit.

15 Bradley T. Lepper, "A Monumental Engine of World Renewal," in Jones and Shields, eds., *The Newark Earthworks*, 41–61.

16 Ray Lively and Robin Horn, "A Grand Unification of Earth, Sky, and Mind," in Jones and Shields, eds., *The Newark Earthworks*, 62–93. This article gives a detailed analysis of the complex geometry of the Great Octagon and Observatory Circle, connecting land and sky.

PART 2: LITTLE VOICES

1 Witness testimony to the Regina Riot Inquiry Commission, cf. Bill Waiser, *All Hell Can't Stop Us: The On-To-Ottawa Trek and Regina Riot* (Fifth House, 2003).

2 Fiona's story. At the time of this writing, survivors, siblings, and members of second and third generations continue to look for victims of the Ideal Maternity Home. They are looking for connections and for closure on a family story. Many are seeking out the truth of their own identities. The compassion behind this difficult, personal work is one of the few points of redemption in this darkest of stories.

3 Jerry Rush, *The Bones of Their Occasion* (Cormorant Books, 1986).

PART 3: SONG OF THE LARK

1 2008 Napa Valley Writers' Conference. Workshop leaders were Ron Carlson, Lan Samantha Chang, Ehud Havazelet, Ann Packer, Mark Doty, Nick Flynn, Brenda Hillman, and Claudia Rankine.

2 Louise Bernice Halfe – Sky Dancer, *Burning in This Midnight Dream* (Coteau Books, 2016). Halfe – Sky Dancer served as the Parliamentary Poet Laureate in 2021 and 2022.

3 TRC, Canada's Truth and Reconciliation Commission on the impact of residential school, their abuses, the child deaths, and their role in extinguishing Indigenous language and culture. The hearings were held across Canada over six years, with the final report being published in December 2016, available on the TRC's website: https://nctr.ca/records/reports/#trc-reports.

4 Louise Bernice Halfe – Sky Dancer, "Winter Visitations," in *Burning in This Midnight Dream* (Coteau Books, 2016), 19.

5 Email correspondence with Carla Harris, October 8, 2022.

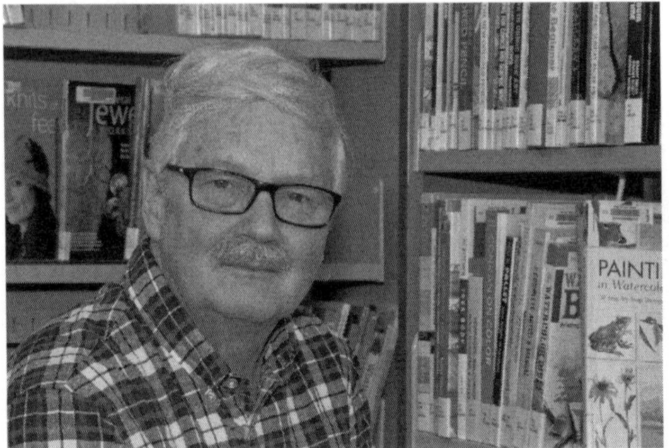
PHOTO BY DENNIS J. EVANS.

Bruce Rice is a Saskatchewan Poet Laureate (2019–2021), an essayist, and editor. His writing moves from family and community to social history and meditations on landscape and wilderness. Bruce's six books of poetry have received two Saskatchewan Book Awards and a Saskatchewan Book of the Year nomination. His first book, *Daniel,* won the Canadian Authors Association Award. Judges said it "portrays life's hardships with an elegance of language which is stunning." He has been called a master of light. Whether writing about prairie or the urban forest outside his door, he says, "I became a better poet when I surrendered to beauty." Bruce lives in Regina on Treaty 4 Territory and the Métis homeland.